Obey the Vision

Keith Gerner

New Wine Press

New Wine Press
PO Box 17
Chichester PO20 6YB
England

First published 1996

Bible verses are taken from the Holy Bible, New International
Version copyright © 1973, 1978, 1984.
Published by Hodder & Stoughton.

ISBN 1 874367 49 3

Typesetting and editorial by Kingdom Come Trust
Newtownards, Northern Ireland

Printed in England by Clays Ltd, St Ives plc

Contents

Keith and Elsie Gerner

Foreword

"Keith's been such a blessing and inspiration to me", enthused a lady from one of our congregations. She didn't know that I'd planned to write, within a few days, this foreword for Keith Gerner's book. On the other hand, I knew that with such a rich accent, if for no other reason, the lady in question came from the 'Emerald Isle', where Keith and Elsie have been labouring together to extend the Kingdom of God for more than 30 years.

Such a ministry in Ireland has been Keith's prime vision, to which he has sought to be obedient. Of course, it was the apostle Paul who first declared his commitment to Jesus in these terms: *"I was not disobedient to the heavenly vision."* **(Acts 26:19)** Keith has sought, as the scripture teaches, to imitate the apostle in visionary obedience, and without doubt 'obedient commitment' is written over every page of this book.

Keith's story begins in a godly English home, and continues through exciting days in Ireland, with the early Charismatic Renewal and street level evangelism, expressing love for both Protestant and Catholic Irish people alike. Now rooted in the land and people of their adoption, Keith and Elsie share the lessons, experiences and fruit of their international ministry and frequent travels.

Keith's pastoral heart and teaching ability flow through the anecdotes of his own experience. The lessons this book teaches us are hammered out on the anvil of his own life – successes and mistakes alike. I've quoted this over-used metaphor because there has been much of this hammering in Keith's life. He well knows the truth of our Lord's promise in **John 16:33,** "In the world you will have tribulation." The Lord keeps his promise and assures us in the midst of pressure that he has overcome, so be of good cheer. There is much to cheer about in this story.

Adventures of living by faith, when God steps in at the last minute; healings of the seriously ill, which touch the emotions; words of supernatural knowledge, and reconciliation across the divide of religion and race; all jostle together. However, above all, perhaps it's the timely publication of Keith's story which makes this book so relevant. Where will the Charismatic Renewal go?

Is there a future for deepening the first overtures of reconciliation in the midst of sectarian intolerance and violence? Can those who have gladly embraced sacrifice and privation for Jesus' sake ever be understood by those who promote prosperity in Jesus' name? Is the current refreshment of the Spirit revival, or do we "look for another?" Will God fulfil his eschatological promises through ministries unrelated to the life and discipline of the body of Christ?

All these are relevant, current and significant questions and they are raised through Keith's story, which also contributes to the needed answers. Much down to earth wisdom will be gleaned from this biography. "Revival is not for lazy people," and, "It is divine healing not faith healing," are but two salutary and needy nuggets of truth. This wisdom is laced with Keith's dry sense of humour, which could be easily missed. Who would get married on the verse of **1 Samuel 17:10,** *"Give me a man that we may fight together"?* – well, Elsie did!

In addition to all this, I would commend Keith and his story to the church of Christ on two very important points alone:

Firstly, he and Elsie have brought up, in the midst of their very demanding ministry and the trials and pressures of northern Irish life, a lovely family of three believing offspring. Many folk are not aware of the pressure that front-line ministry brings on the family of God's servants. It is the front-line troops who take the full pressure of the enemy, and Christian front-liners are no exception.

The attack often comes through the family. Keith has learned to protect and inspire his two sons and daughter; they all love and serve Keith's master. That is a great commendation, and one we should honour and seek to emulate.

Secondly, there are a large number in full-time ministry today who recognise and gladly confess the influence of Keith's teaching and example, which came to them in the formative and training years of their ministries.

Keith's influence on the generation just coming up behind him is very extensive indeed. This augurs well for Ireland and tells us that Keith certainly didn't get it far wrong. May God help us through Keith's story to also obey the vision He has given us.

Roger Forster
Ichthus, London

Introduction

This is the gripping story of a vision given to Keith Gerner, and worked out through thirty five years of ministry in Ireland. The vision was based on reading, in **John 3:34**, that God is prepared to give the Holy Spirit without measure to individual believers in the last days, and that Churches could be formed, supernaturally supplied and directed by the Holy Ghost.

This book is written to show the history of the formation of a totally new kind of Church, which has survived civil war, and has passed from being a prophetic dream to practical reality. It is an inspiring account of a dream that came true and has answers for the world today.

After an early experience of God in childhood, Keith gives a first hand account of the amazing revival in Ireland after his journey in faith, through professional ministry training in England, to a place of total dependence on God, to bless the whole Church.

After a period of school teaching, where he saw

God work in power among children, God brought him into a modern Pentecost when he heard Latin spoken in tongues, praising the blood of Christ. He became one of the pioneers of the 'body ministry' of supernatural gifts, after spending extensive time in fasting and prayer for revival.

His experience in country areas with Catholic people at the time of the Civil Rights marches, was followed by his association with a dozen praying people who were there at the beginning of the all-Ireland Charismatic Movement, which peaked in an International Conference in Dublin in the 1970s, with well over seventy thousand attending.

The problems associated with this move are honestly faced by Keith, including mistakes which he himself made, and he suggests that renewal and revival are not the same thing. He shares how the formation of a new kind of church has become possible through cell-group meetings, where people in Ireland have begun to simply gather as 'Christians' – rather than Catholics or Protestants.

The impact of this move, and the working out of this new, supernaturally-empowered church – which may have to face new challenges in the days ahead – led on to his present position as a world teacher, travelling to America, Australia and the Far East.

This book will inspire those who wish to know how the church can survive through troubled times, and who have a vision of what God wants for His people in the days ahead, because it is written from practical experience, based on Scriptural principles.

The book is intended as a testimony to the grace

and power of the Lord Jesus Christ through some dark days of human history, bringing real hope and objectives for praying people.

Christ's vision and prayer saved Peter from suicide in **Luke 22**, and we trust this book will inspire praying Christians at a critical time in world history. "Without a vision, people perish," (**Proverbs 29:18 KJV**), but we trust this book will provide hope for those in despair and a practical manual for those who wish to see the church blessed in the days ahead.

1

Birth of the Vision

Where there is no vision, people perish. I knew that night in Newry Town Hall in 1972, that, short of a miracle, I would not get out alive. Life was cheap then in Northern Ireland, and violent men had entered the meeting.

The Town Hall had not had such a meeting for half a century. Suddenly a woman, blind in one eye, moved forward. "I want my vision restored," she faltered, "and I am believing God for a healing." Ten minutes later, God gave us a miracle and she began to see.

One hundred and twenty people found the same power in new vision for their life in the next few nights, and my own life was saved – in spite of those dangerous men at the meetings. Once again, I had proved the power of being obedient to the vision God had given for a nation-wide miracle.

Within eight years, I was to see the whole of Ireland radically changed by that same vision. A world gathering in Dublin, of seventy-six thousand believers, sprang from a praying group of twelve people. In Ireland, only God could have given such a vision, and brought about the Charismatic Movement,

In 1969, He warned some praying people that blood was going to be spilt across the land, and that time was short. It was because of that, that I began increasingly to move away from the city of Belfast, with its many healing meetings, into country areas. This process brought us to Rathfriland, in Co. Down.

There eighteen people made decisions for Christ in one week, yet God said to me, "I don't want you to stay here. I want you to go to Newry." When I asked the Town Clerk, "When did you last have a mission in Newry?" he said, "Years ago, in 1922, with Mr W. P. Nicholson."

I said, "Well, why have there been no other missions?"

"Mr. Gerner," said the clerk, and he looked me straight in the face, "Have you heard of the unrest in this town?"

I replied, "No."

"Well," he said, "I have to warn you that you may well have some dangerous people at your meetings."

Nevertheless, in February, we began with a Healing Crusade. I had a definite burden for the Catholic people. On the second night, violent men entered the meeting. That same night the lady who was blind in one eye was healed. Because of the supernatural miracle, I was protected from the violent men who were there.

During this crusade, the Lord showed me that only a miraculous manifestation of God's power could save the province from bloodshed. I determined in my heart to go to every country town in Northern Ireland with this message. With miracles, however, came the challenge of the counterfeit Spiritist move. At Newry, I had found a strong connection with Spiritism.

Immediately we experienced conflict. One person, when they wrote away for Faith Healing – not Divine Healing – had had the ghost of their dead uncle appear at the bottom of their bed. He had to renounce this action, and we had to plead the cleansing power of the blood of Christ, before he was set free from oppression and permanently healed. Divine healing glorifies Christ and is permanent, whereas spirit healing can be temporary and brings glory to another.

After Newry, every month or so, we began to take major public halls in towns around Northern Ireland, with the message that Christ is alive today, to forgive and heal. In God's economy, a tremendous thing began to happen – from Newry round to Enniskillen, Omagh and Londonderry, we proclaimed the power of God in large towns. These were destined to see some of the worst bloodshed in the Civil Rights fighting, with bombs and bullets, in the years that followed in Ulster – yet by this means the Lord gave these people a chance to turn to Him first, for eternal peace and life in Christ.

In one town, we saw an unbelieving woman healed. Suddenly, I noticed 'supernatural oil' appeared in the hand of my friend, Ernie Busby – who was a local pig farmer. The lady had proudly announced at the beginning of the meeting, "Nobody will get me to believe this sort of thing." After prayer, she was able to hear through a totally deaf ear!

This does not mean that we had great faith. Personally, I was scared to go to Londonderry on 25th-28th June, because the hall was only five hundred yards from the Bogside, which was a centre of terrorist activity. It was only the grace of God that allowed us to go to this great city.

In a mission at Fintona, Co. Tyrone, God spoke to me out of **Acts 18:9**, *"I have much people in this city, be not afraid."* On the first night in Derry, a lady came who suffered from multiple sclerosis. After prayer, she stood up and walked out of her wheelchair – healed!

In such a wonderful way did God show his power, that both Catholics and Protestants thronged the Guild-hall to give the glory to the risen Christ. In fact, God moved powerfully. That year alone, two thousand people came to Jesus Christ for forgiveness and healing. The miracles of the Holy Spirit were going out to the poor. The Lord Jesus Himself was anointed to help such people, **(Luke 4:18)** – His ministry is to continue, with us doing the same as He did.

Meanwhile, in answer to prayer, God was working in a sovereign way among Roman Catholics, for an even greater change. David du Plessis – from South Africa and the USA – later told me that he, personally, had been present when the leadership of the Catholic Church revised its attitude to Protestants – now 'separated brethren'. Following this move – around the same time that Israel became a nation – God began to bless some American Catholics with the gifts of the Holy Spirit.

So, revival was linked historically to those two great events. There is a timing with the Spirit. It is God, not we, Who fixes the programme. Our part is to make sure we do not miss it. Certainly, in Pentecostal churches in Ireland, this new move came as a surprise. As often happened in past revival, the difficulties of the new move came mainly from the old.

The Charismatic Renewal certainly involved one of the traditional Pentecostal leaders, David Du Plessis. He was world secretary of the Pentecostal Churches. At that time, his philosophy was, "Well, God will forget about the old, dead churches and the new church will be formed out of Pentecostals."

One day, David was driving along with a friend, when a train rammed into their car at great speed. When he came round, he found that his bones were broken, but he had no pain. The doctors said that they couldn't understand this, but David sensed that God had 'stopped him in his tracks', as it were, to give him a new vision.

God told him that he was to go to the World Council of Churches. "What?" said David, "Those that do not take a firm stand on Your Word in the bible? I can't compromise." "I don't want you to compromise," the Lord said, "I want you to testify." "But they're enemies," replied David. "Well," said the Lord, "I did say to love your enemies." **(Matthew 5:44)**

David knew he had to obey God, and he found that he had been healed. When he went to testify about his experience of being Baptised in the Spirit in 1935, he also remembered that, about that same time, Smith Wigglesworth – another Pentecostal leader – had told him that the world would see a tremendous outpouring of the Holy Spirit.

Meanwhile, among Roman Catholics, Pope John had been elected. He had a simple peasant background – he loved the Lord and sought God in prayer. The Lord Jesus appeared to him and said that he would revive the church, but he must hold the General

17

Council – known since as **Vatican II**.

When this was called together, David du Plessis was invited over. He gave the advice that the Lord wanted every Catholic to read the bible. The acceptance of this advice proved to be a vital key to blessing with us in Ireland. In the south of Ireland, bibles began to be read. Meanwhile, as a result of Catholics changing their attitude to Martin Luther, Protestants – who had been 'heretics' – now became 'separated brethren'. What a radical change!

In the north of Ireland also, things began to happen. One Roman Catholic, who lived in Belfast, had a cafe next door to a member of the Elim Pentecostal Church. This Elim man shared with him about the baptism of the Holy Spirit, and how Catholics were being blessed in America.

The Catholic man went to his friend's Elim Pastor and said, "I want to be baptised in the Spirit – I've been to Mass, I've said my Hail Marys and now I'm all ready for the baptism. I'm as spiritual as I can be!"

The pastor, an Englishman, said, "You'd better go away and we'll pray about it for a week." What he really thought was, "What is this guy saying? How can I be sure of him? Salvation and baptism in the Spirit come by a free gift from God, not as a reward for religious activity."

The man was a little disappointed, but went home and threw open his bible. He read **John 3:30,** *"I must decrease, and he must increase."* He decided he would come as he was and give his life to the Lord, and accept God's Spirit as a free gift. And, of course, when he came back, the Elim pastor was wonderfully blessed by this. Without hesitation, he laid hands on him to pray, and the man began to praise God loudly in tongues!

This Catholic was now rejoicing in Christ, but was not ready to immediately leave his own Church. He was told that he would not be welcome among Pentecostals at that time unless he did so. When he wanted to know where he could go for teaching, he wrote to America and they wrote back, "There's a person called Keith Gerner, who has meetings in the Queen's University area with Mrs. Irwin."

So this Roman Catholic man came to us at the house meeting. He was delighted that we were holding a teaching meeting, with bible studies on tape. Then he said, casually, "Can I bring some people up from Dublin – including a Roman Catholic priest?"

That challenged me! I had a lot of support from the Protestant Shankill Road. With all these Protestant people I faced the destruction of my reputation and the price to be paid in lost financial support – and God had already taken me out of the Anglo-Catholic system. Yet for the sake of the new vision God was giving – of a revival among Roman Catholic people – I decided to risk my position with my Protestant friends.

In fact, we lost eighteen hundred pounds of income that year, as people withdrew their backing from us. Revival does not come without someone paying a price, but the rewards in blessing far outweighed the cost. (Mark 10:30)

By January 1973, many Catholics were coming into the blessings of Pentecost. During our visit to Dublin, in December, we had contacted over three hundred now interested in this move – at the beginning of the year there had only been twelve.

We were impressed by: an awareness of deep prayer life – one sister praying for us in the north from 5 am!; a great interest in reading the Word of God; and a real desire for fellowship with God's people. **(1 John 3:14)**

I told my Roman Catholic friend in Belfast that I would like to go down to the south of Ireland, and have a weekend convention. He replied, "We'd like you to take on Gormanstown" – a large place near Mosney, run by the Catholic Franciscan Order.

Who would be the keynote speaker, acceptable to my new friends? After prayer, I felt that only one man could do this – somebody who was Pentecostal, and whom Catholics would accept – David du Plessis.

To bring him over from America, I faced a huge bill – and with decreasing funds. I wrote to him anyway. He graciously replied that he was coming across to London and could easily fly to Ireland, so I would only have to pay for his air flight from London. Although he did not know me, David, also, came in faith.

Of course, as soon as his name was announced, many Catholics flocked to Gormanston College, Co. Meath, in the south of Ireland – a Franciscan boys school. This was our watershed conference – 27th-30th April, 1973. The Principal was quite open-minded, although he did say, "Don't use the chapel, as it's consecrated. If you want to pray for people, use the gymnasium. If you want to immerse people, you can use the swimming pool – tongue in the cheek – but don't let me know."

At that point, the leader of the Full Gospel Businessmen's Fellowship International – whom I knew from the north, and who was raised in a staunch

Protestant, Orange Order background – said, "I'll come for half an hour to hear this man, and that is only because I know you are sound." He brought along some of his friends, and they stayed – for the full three days!

Meanwhile, the cleaner of the Catholic College came up, while we were setting up the equipment. Suddenly, as in **Psalm 45:7,** we smelt the fragrance of Jesus in the room. "Where is this incense coming from?" she asked – even she sensed a miracle.

That afternoon, seventeen of the nuns and priests received life-changing visions. They spoke in tongues and came into experience of the gifts of the Spirit. Since then, some have gone abroad with this vision – some of them are now writing to me from Africa. Revival and mission go together. Ireland's exports include people.

The impact upon me was profound. I had left the Anglo-Catholic system without bitterness. Now came a new vision of ministry, to join people as 'Christians'. We thanked God for the miracle of Gormanston, where over two hundred gathered from every part of Ireland – both clergy and laity of every major denomination.

As David du Plessis ministered in the power of the Holy Spirit, Christ was uplifted as Saviour, Healer, Baptiser and coming King. The immediate miracles of healing and forgiveness were followed by an impact on the whole community.

For example, one sister had a personal vision of Christ there; another brother wrote to say that sixty boys in his Catholic school had received Christ as Saviour – forty of them had already begun to speak in heavenly languages, being given visions of a mighty move of God ahead.

Despite the extensive bible reading, prayer and assurance of personal contact with Christ, which was experienced in the south, there was still deep suspicion in the north about 'counterfeits' and 'superstition'. Many were discovering the bible for the first time, and we tried to help them with teaching tapes and bible study courses.

When we returned to the north and were praying for Ireland, the Lord very graciously gave us a vision of the mighty army of Joel – all dressed in white – sweeping across Ireland in a great move of the Holy Spirit. (Joel 2:5-9) We were clearly shown at the time, however, that a move of this sort would depend upon everyone getting into place and keeping rank, in step with one another.

Some Shankill Road elders of the Protestant church I was attending at the time, came to see me – "We cannot understand where God is leading you, Keith, but we know your character over the years, and I want you to know that we trust you." Thank God for those in every denomination with the bigger vision of Christ's Kingdom.

Sadly, I also attended a major conference of Spirit-filled pastors, who solemnly voted that this new Charismatic Movement was "a counterfeit of the enemy" – because Roman Catholics were not leaving their church to become Protestants.

The devil also introduced a new attack in the spirit realm – with the film, "The Exorcist" – which was widely screened across Ulster. Significantly, when I was interviewed on national television, a clip of this film was shown, in which the mother of the demon-possessed child asked, "How do I know that my child is possessed?" and the Exorcist replied, "Does she speak in tongues?" I had to explain that a counterfeit can only be viable where there is first a genuine experience.

We now faced the task of spiritual warfare for all of Northern Ireland. This meant co-ordinating witness to thousands of young people and old, who were flocking to see this new film. We were told that, each week of that November, forty thousand people went to see the brutal story of demon possession and the suicide of the priest. This had led already to some people taking their own lives in England.

With the advent of 'The Exorcist', we realised we had been called to shoulder a leading responsibility, to help the many young people who were hungry for the supernatural at that time. When a prayer chain for that film was started, numbers dropped dramatically at the cinema, and the number of contacts grew.

We were reminded by the Lord that He had put us in Ireland because we love the people, and that we have a responsibility to share what He has given us in the realm of teaching materials and gifts. Of course, we also made our own mistakes. David du Plessis was very balanced in what he put forward, but the Charismatic Renewal began to emphasise Church sacraments, naming them "baptism in the Spirit".

The Lord was faithful, however, in warning us about more dangers. He gave us a vision of pure water coming down, at which animals were drinking. We saw that the bigger animals were pushing the smaller ones. God was warning us that the leadership of the revival would pass from the praying people to organising, pushy political people. A friend of mine, from Newry, received the same vision independently – at a conference where the Charismatic leaders formed an organising committee to run the new movement.

There were problems inside the movement as well as outside, as people tried to put "new wine into an old wineskin." (Matthew 9:17) Finally, my own role in the whole process was brought into question. My prophet friend from England telephoned me and said, "The new leaders are going to push you out, as they do not accept your apostolic role, but cheer up, "the stone which the builders rejected," is still useful to God." (Luke 20:17) That happened with the new leaders the following week!

All the original people – like the Belfast Roman Catholic who had shared with us at Queen's – kept up their friendship with me, because they realised that we had actually prayed this move in, and were not looking for power or position from the move of God.

There is a price to pay for vision when you first see it, a further cost when you are in it, and a final process of death, whereby God can bring you to His next move. God is always moving forward and creating new vision from the old one. Man often wishes merely to stay put in blessing, without radical change. How did this happen to the new leaders? They wanted acceptability for this revival with the 'established Church'. The Church wanted organisation which did not 'rock the boat'.

Leaders began to say to people, "There's nothing

new really, you're just coming into what the Church has always taught" – and so they tried to contain the new wine. The Lord Jesus warned about this. (**Mark 2:22**) He laid aside His reputation to bring redemption. (**Philippians 2:7**)

At that time, my English prophet friend received a significant vision of a cat. God showed him a tabby cat, able to fly and disappear supernaturally. When this animal was introduced to a larger tabby cat – sitting firmly on the ground in one corner – the latter swallowed up and destroyed the supernatural animal. The new cat, the Spirit-led church, had the markings of the old cat, the traditional church, but unless the new move remained free, it would be swallowed up by the administration of the 'old establishment'.

God wants us to walk personally with Him through danger, in blind trust. (**Isaiah 42:16**) Some in the old system, however, caught the new vision. At the Gormanston Conference there was, for instance, a nun in a red trouser suit – which was a real challenge to my 'traditional' mind – and a young priest in training, who was subsequently posted to Limerick.

At his invitation, a Protestant friend of mine, who had a healing ministry, went down to Limerick to pray for the sick, and had a big impact in healings. This priest then called us to meet some traditional ministers and have a joint conference in the Limerick school, at Easter 1975.

We went down, and I spoke on the baptism in the Spirit, while a Spirit-filled priest spoke on the value of salvation from St. Paul's Epistle to the Romans. Another priest was sitting in the congregation commenting loudly on the priest's message, "This is Lutheranism." When I spoke, his comment was, "This is Protestantism."

I suggested he come along to the afternoon seminar on the Gifts of the Spirit. The first priest out for prayer was this same critic, who had wanted "nothing to do with it." He said, "I want salvation, I want to be baptised in the Spirit. I want healing for my face." The Lord answered his request and he received everything – his face was healed of psoriasis, he spoke in tongues. He was so changed that people in open air meetings would hear him speaking and say, "Father, lay off, you're too hot for us." We heard this six months later.

The Holy Spirit is wonderfully patient and gracious in His dealings. The whole of our family were engaged in this marvellous outpouring. At Limerick, our Gareth, just ten years old, went around praying in tongues behind his Dad. As we began to pray for someone who was in need, this person said, "I want the wee fellow to pray for me and put his hands on my head," and nothing would do until Gareth had prayed.

God was present when, like small children, we ministered in the west of Ireland, both town and country alike. Humility was the essence of Charismatic revival. How did this affect Ireland? Peace did not come – but people were changed.

In June 1975, I told my praying friends the story of Chris Mein, an ex-alcoholic, who was anointed to sing in our crusade meetings. He came home to find his son filled with bullets from Catholic terrorists – simply for being in the wrong place at the wrong time. That night he hugged the Catholic priest in our meeting. After that he announced the title of his song for that meeting, "My heavenly father watches over me." There were few dry eyes as he sang.

His boy had so recently become part of the tragedy of Ulster, and yet in the revival, Chris could sincerely sing these words. Only real faith and real power from the Holy Spirit could have made such a testimony possible. Easter celebrations became real as a result. We saw the way that Christ is able to heal individuals, in homes which are perfectly committed to Him.

I believe that the love, generated by the Charismatic Movement, could have healed the nation if the response had been there from all of God's people. Just like the Jews – who preferred civil war to the loving ministry of the Lord Jesus, and suffered annihilation under the Romans in AD 70 – so God lovingly pleaded with His people. (Luke 13:34) A hardening of the heart, and lack of forgiveness, led inevitably to His judgement.

Suspicious Ireland did not change, and was to suffer this for twenty-five years afterwards. It is better to bend to the wind, than be broken by it. New converts cannot be expected to suddenly change their culture, although they may be deeply affected by the Spirit – yet they were expected to do so in Ireland.

For example, we were praying in a house in a little country place near Limerick, when someone said he wanted to be baptised in the Spirit. After prayer, he collapsed on the floor, speaking in tongues. Later, a friend of mine from the north of Ireland said that he thought this Roman Catholic should join a Protestant church. Everybody laughed, because there was no living Protestant nearby – this was in the middle of a southern Irish bog.

Meanwhile, the southern man was saying, "I want to experience heaven again, like I just did. Can you arrange another trip for me tomorrow?" I said to my northern friend, "What's the point of opening up a Protestant church, when all these people are Christians, with bibles, meeting in homes in a New Testament way?" Similar blindness overtook my other northern friends, who thought the whole movement was a 'deception of the devil' – despite a very gracious explanation by my Anglican friend, Rev. Cecil Kerr, of Rostrevor, that bible reading was spreading.

I must admit, on that occasion, that I enjoyed the remarks of an apostolic pastor, who commented, "Five thousand bibles sold as a result of the Charismatic Movement? Gentleman, I believe, if this revival is of the Devil, he must just have been converted!" This pastor, unlike many other traditional Pentecostal leaders, had a broad vision of the Kingdom of God, and was a missionary apostle of mature standing, who started thousands of African churches.

There are, of course, faults on both sides. Younger converts sometimes look down on their older counterparts, and do not understand their needs. A loving Dublin group arranged a 'Holy Hooley' for me, when I happened to be tired, which went on until two o'clock in the morning, and were surprised when I then asked them to close the meeting by singing the 'Our Father'. They meant well, but ...

The renewal people did not want to be called 'Pentecostal', so they made up a name –

'Charismatic'. In its turn, 'Charismatic' became debased into a term commonly used to describe anyone with strong personality. In order to escape this, new terms were introduced like, 'Christian' or, 'the new move of God'.

Like children, new converts realise the shortcomings of their parents, and fall into the same traps. Each new vision can only benefit, if it humbly honours real maturity. Sometimes vision also brings new structure. We had to learn that the old wineskin is not always able to stretch enough to accommodate the new wine, no matter how much folk wanted to do this in Ireland. Nevertheless, thank God, the old Book of Acts became a living book – people began to read the bible.

What main teachings emerged?

First, when they read through the book of Acts, they found that the disciples met in houses.

Secondly, they saw that Christ was going to come back for his Bride, and the Bride had to be the same Church He had left in miraculous power. In Acts, they found that they had to attend the temple. People say, "Why don't people come out?" Well, why did the early Christians stay in? Annas and Caiaphas had just crucified Jesus, and there were Peter and John, merrily going up and down to the Temple, and worshipping daily – in an outdated Jewish system. They stayed in to witness – though, eventually, in **Acts 7**, they were thrown out.

Although the witnessing was in the temple, the breaking of bread, fellowship and teaching took place in the homes. (**Acts 2: 42**) Finally, the move of God outgrew Judaism altogether, and led to a world vision.

Thank God for this result in the Charismatic revival, which has led to a greater vision of God's world plan for the last days, before the Lord returns.

In the midst of 'the troubles', we caught a new vision – that it was possible to have a totally supernatural church, awaiting the return of the Lord, full of the Spirit – like the five wise virgins in **Matthew 25**. This was something that sustained Christians through these years in Ireland.

What was the essence of the vision? – based on **John 3:34,** that the Lord is prepared to give, to all His people, all the gifts of the Holy Ghost, without measure.

2

Home and Family

What was the background to this vision? How did it come in the first place?

The vision was given to my parents, even before I came to birth. I do thank God for a praying father and mother. My father was brought up in a Baptist family. When he was growing up, he wanted to become a missionary – particularly to China. The board turned him down on health grounds – and yet he was accepted by the British Army in 1914 as an officer!

My father was trained as a Civil Engineer and was involved in the building of Hull docks. During the war, he was gassed in the fighting. He returned home, more unfit for the mission field than ever before. He settled into his father's firm, but still felt the call of God to mission work.

He became one of the founder members of BYMM – the Baptist Young Men's Movement – and felt this was a measure of what God was asking him to do. Because he saw that he could not fulfil the missionary emphasis upon his life, he determined that this same vision would be fulfilled in the life of his child.

From the moment of my conception, therefore, this vision – of reaching those without Christ – was prayed into my life. My father dedicated me to the Lord before I was born. Holy Ghost vision comes through prayer. It has been wonderful to inherit so much from my family, and to know that the grace of God has been released into my life through their intercession.

A Holy Spirit vision, born in prayer, gently leads – rather than pushes. The parental key is prayer and not human manipulation. My father released me as his child to find my own bent and calling in God – as a result, the Lord Jesus Christ has appeared to me on three occasions.

Christ gave me His own calling to a life of service, in the midst of a civil war situation in Ulster. Like Paul, because we have not been disobedient to the heavenly vision, we have found divine protection – though over three thousand have died here in these last years.

My mother, Julia Gerner, was converted under Dr. Shields in Toronto – in a fundamental Baptist church. She came to England, where she was commended to the care of W.I. Fullerton. She met my father in Baptist circles, and they were married soon afterwards.

My father was still very attached to his own family and their first house was very close to the family home. My mother, about the time of my birth, felt close to breakdown and wanted to move away. They took another house which backed onto a golf course.

My father, who was working in the Corn Exchange in London, was still in the family business and was away quite a bit of the time.

My mother sensed God's call on my life and wanted to send me to school, and later to University, with a view to professional Anglican ministry. She sent me to a boarding school in Kent, where I gained a scholarship to another school in Dorset. This was in 1939, during the German bombing blitz.

While I was there, the conflict between my father's sister and my mother drove my father to the verge of collapse. His sister had helped financially in putting him through much of his college training, and the relationship had continued to be close. While he was recuperating in a nursing home, it received a direct hit from a German bomb – all that was left to identify the body was his wedding ring!

For many years my mother was still waiting for him to turn up. Thus, uncertainty and loss hung over all our lives for a considerable period of time. Because my own father was blown to pieces by a bomb, I can identify with many people who have suffered through troubles and persecution, and the uncertainty of those whose loved-ones have suddenly disappeared.

God gave mother an answer by looking after her, (Isaiah 54:5), and, for me, He also took the place of my father. My mother put on my father's tombstone in London, the significant words, "Called to higher service."

Because of the conflict with her sister-in-law, my mother was reduced in circumstances and went to live near Bude in Cornwall. When I was six or seven, my mother's sister in Canada, Aunt Dorothy, who was an active Christian, sent me the book, 'How Derek Won his Way'. It was a Christian book about a young boy who was challenged to read a bible verse, **Revelation 3:2**, "Here I am. I stand at the door and knock. If anyone hears my voice and opens the door, I will come in and eat with him, and he with me."

This verse was illustrated with a picture of Jesus standing at the door, with no outside handle. It had to be opened, not from the outside, but from the inside. Now, although my father and mother were Christians, I had to make my own decision to come to the Lord. No outside family influence was enough to make me new in Christ. I noticed that He stands at the door and knocks. He did not force his way into my life. I opened up my heart and life and asked the Lord to come in through simple prayer – then I knew He had kept His promise to change me from inside.

Immediately, I encountered a problem – because, like my wife, Elsie, I was brought up in a Christian home, there was little change in my behaviour after receiving the Lord into my life. I simply believed He had come in, because the promise was given in His word. I know that other people have also had this problem, asking, "Am I truly a Christian?" You cannot just depend upon your emotions. Look instead at the promise of God, **(Revelation 3:20)**, "If anyone opens the door, I will come in."

Faith is based not on feelings, but the fact that God does not lie. **(Numbers 23:19)** As I began to read, the Lord also showed me that I could now know that He was mine and I was His. Eternal life is something you have right here and now. In **1 John 5:12,13** the bible promises, "He who has the Son, has life." It is not a one-time experience – not, "had the Son," but, "has the Son" – it's a daily walk with the Lord. "He who does not have the Son of God, does not have life."

You can be born in a Christian home – that does not make you a Christian. We all have to make our own personal contact with Christ, and then go on in fellowship with Him – (**1 John 5:13**), "I write these things to you, who believe in the name of the Son of God, that you may know that you have eternal life." Notice the tenses here. It is a continuous daily knowledge – of having eternal life now, as we walk in unbroken contact with Christ. Our future is secure, as we go on daily with Him.

When it came time to leave the junior school and go on to the high school, there was a traditional service in the school chapel. The boys leaving the school each picked a hymn to be sung. As a definite dedication of my life, I remember choosing John Bunyan's pilgrim hymn:

There's no discouragement,
Shall make him once relent,
His first avowed intent,
To be a pilgrim.

At that time, I wasn't aware of the rejection, the problems, and even the danger, that would attend my life for the next thirty five years. But I still do not regret making that decision. I can still sing and mean those words. There were some immediate challenges, however, in working it out.

The bitterness between my mother and her sister-in-law continued to such an extent that my mother reverted to her maiden name of Gerner. This created a problem at my next school, because I had won a scholarship in my previous surname. The boys came up to me to ask, "How did you get a scholarship when your name's not on the board?" That was a bit difficult to explain for a young kid.

My mother had also decided to make sacrifices – such as taking in guests to her house – so that I could be a boarder at the next school, where I would obtain the training, which she knew I needed, to fulfil my call to the ministry.

Everybody knew I had this call – even my headmaster wrote of, "A very strong sense of dedication." I used to win bible knowledge prizes at school – although that was more because nobody else had much of a clue, than on account of my extensive knowledge of Scripture!

Possibly, because of this lack of parental contact, I became a very hard worker. I ran many of the school societies at one time or another. I took up chess – playing it blindfolded – and became secretary of the Debating Society for a time. This gave me training in presentation and public speaking.

When I was fifteen, I took up drama. The school play at the time was Shakespeare's, 'Macbeth', and I was one of the three witches. An oratory prize followed for one of my witch's speeches – fine training for preaching! In my exams, I received Distinctions for the various subjects taken. Originally, at the age of nine, as my mother had high ideas of my getting a Classical education, she had sent me to special Greek classes.

From the age of ten, I had been translating English verse into Latin verse, and began to discover a gifting for writing verses and poetry. I contributed to the school magazines, also – but mostly anonymously. Then my mother decided that the circulation in my hands was bad. She taught me typing as a form of exercise. From an early age, I did a lot of typing. This helped to develop my interest in research.

Although, at fifteen, I had passed through my junior exams, the Classics master suggested I wouldn't go on to Oxford unless I improved my knowledge of Greek grammar. He recommended that I should switch from Greek to another subject – History. This new course meant two years' study of history in one year.

The school felt that to take on prefectship as well would take too much out of me. They avoided making me a leader, so as to free me to study. This registered, unfortunately, in my young mind as, "I'm not fit for leadership" – an impression that dogged me for many years.

How important are early impressions. I worked very hard, but coming up to the last term, the head-master gave a report to Oxford that I wasn't brilliant scholarship material. They were going to let me take the scholarship anyway, because it was the main way to gain entrance to a particular college.

My mother was furious at this. She determined to show my headmaster that, despite the stiff competition for places, I would succeed. She was certainly tested. There came a crisis at the school – an infectious disease which meant that the whole school had to be quarantined. It was obvious that, if I caught the disease, I would not be able to sit the Oxford exams. I was sent home, so that I wouldn't be quarantined.

At home, mother had to hire a history teacher, who made me write all sorts of essays and work hard – praying at the same time. My mother had real faith in God, that He could work miracles.

When we were living in Sevenoaks, my brother Malcolm had been subjected to very severe headaches, connected with hydrocephalus – water on the brain. The V-bombs were coming over at the time. He was put into hospital to undergo an operation – a very delicate process, involving drilling the skull to relieve the pressure.

My mother received a verse from God, "I am the Lord, Who healeth thee." **(Exodus 15:26)** In faith, she signed him out of hospital. Of the other people who had the operation, some died, and some of them became insane. My brother was then taken to Canada by my mother. He seems to have been completely healed – later, he became an art teacher in Dundas, Ontario.

Meanwhile, back at school, I was amazed to hear that I had won an open scholarship. Not content with that, the Lord also gave me a Distinction in the History paper, so I found myself with a county scholarship from the west of England – where we were living – a state scholarship, and an open scholarship. All these gave me about six hundred pounds' worth of scholarship, plus all the relevant clothing allowances – so that all our needs were met!

This was quite a contrast to life at home. At Exmoor, we lived a lot by prayer. We had no money or food, sometimes, so we trapped rabbits and dug potatoes, in order to survive. It was quite a struggle as a family. We were being educated that God is our Healer and Provider, in a practical way.

For the last school term, my mother had said that she didn't have the money to send me to school. She prayed in secret and Jesus appeared to her in the hall. That very day we had two cheques for twice the money that was needed. Then God granted me – at the age of seventeen, these scholarships to Oxford University.

This was my first real experience of financial miracles. We had another stage of great debt when they came to lift everything – furniture and all. A Christian woman was sent to us by God. She said, "There's an old caravan which you have lying in the back, I'll buy it," and that took us out of debt, on the brink of disaster.

These childhood experiences have never left me. This has been the simple way in which I have learnt that God can meet material needs in answer to sincere prayer. In fact, since my father was blown to pieces, God has given me a precious promise – that He would be my father, if I, through Christ, would be His son.

People say to me, "Keith, I've been neglected by my father, neglected by my mother. My family do not want me. What is the answer to that problem?" The first answer is to forgive, if there is bitterness.

The second, is not to go seeking for affirmation, but to rest in God's promise, (**Mark 10:30**), "If you give up father, mother, children, for my sake and the gospel's, you will not fail to receive a hundred times in this present age, and in the age to come, eternal life." This is not just a promise of eternal life later, but something for here and now.

As we travel the world, we are finding that we're part of a great family, where everyone is brother and sister, mother and father. If there is rejection, or you've had a problem in the past, know that God can give you a family. Get attached to a loving church. Get committed. I have found that out of these relationships, the Lord can bring healing for the past.

Thirdly, without apology, I believe that it's important to know the bible. You must know this book. From a very early age at school, when I had given my life to the Lord, I valued the bible. I have been wonderfully, wonderfully blessed by the word of God. Time and again, it has given me something to stand on. In the mornings, I read the bible first, so that I have something to pray about, and a promise to claim. Often I challenge God, "Lord, you've given me this promise."

When I came to Ireland, He said, "I will give you the heathen for your inheritance." **(Psalm 2:8)** In the last thirty years, we have seen thousands of decisions for Jesus Christ, terminally ill people raised up, and many healed, through trusting this promise.

For a while, I forgot the second part of the promise, "... and the uttermost part of the earth for your possession," **(Psalm 2:8)**, but this also is now real to us, as we travel the world in the Lord's service.

Given a definite promise from the Scripture, in answer to prayer, God will give miracles beyond your wildest dreams. One of my aunts, on my wife's side of the family, Auntie Elsie, was diagnosed as full of cancer. The doctors said they could do nothing for her – they would do the best they could, but her case was terminal. She got up that morning to read the Word. At that time she was one of many Christians who did not believe that healing continues today by Spiritual Gifts – but she was given that verse, "This sickness is not unto death, but for the glory of God." **(John 11:4)**

We buried her just five years ago and I helped carry the coffin. The post-mortem proved no trace of cancer in her body at that time. She had lived for twenty-five years since being diagnosed as 'terminal'. That is not bad for a Christian who did not believe in gifts of healing today!

Unfortunately, after leaving school, I had begun a course of education that would make me doubt this simple faith in the bible. Obviously, with the scholarship, I was set up for Oxford, and my mother then went to Canada.

At this time National Service was compulsory, and all young men had to do two years military service. I decided to do mine in the army. Mother had talked to a person from Winsford, who was related to the Chaplain in Chief. He suggested that I arrange to do six months in Aldershot – which was very strong on military drill – and take up shorthand. I would then be drafted to secretarial work among Chaplains – God had already in view that I should go to the Chaplain's department. So, after I had received my shorthand and typing qualifications, they drafted me, for the rest of my National Service, to the Army Chaplain's Centre.

After coming out of that, I entered Oxford. During the vacations, I stayed with the Franciscan community at Cerne Abbas in Dorset. As a result of going through all the Catholic sacraments – mass, confession, the nine offices – I really went up to Oxford as a High Church person – with a fairly devout background, but without trust in the bible as inspired totally by God. I had become a devout follower of church tradition – but God was about to do something radical in my life.

3

A Student at Oxford.

When I entered Oxford, I came under the High Church system – with a tremendous challenge to my earlier faith in God's Word. They suggested I go to CACTM – the organisation that ran a selection weekend for training of Anglican clergy. I had previously been involved with them in my military work and they endorsed my call to ministry. In my first year at Oxford, I went into the SCM – Student Christian Movement. At the time, SCM did not stand for a literal interpretation of scripture, unlike the Christian Union.

At that stage, by the grace of God, I met a girl training as a doctor, who had been raised in a traditional Methodist church. She shared how she had been asked to go on a mission and was told that she would give her testimony – she did not even know what to say! She got quickly to her knees and gave her life to Christ. Then she began to read her bible and believe it. I could see, as she spoke, that there was a real vitality, which I had lost. Because of this, I began to seek the Lord afresh, from a personal point of view.

I also now began to go to the Scripture Union meetings. At these meetings, I experienced my first revival. First, I found assurance of being definitely saved. I went to a lunch-time prayer meeting and the person leading it read out the verse from **1 Thessalonians 5:9,** "God did not appoint us to suffer wrath, but to receive salvation." I had been praying for God to show me how I stood with Him. That word brought me immediate assurance. This was a whole new vision of intimate relationship with God.

Now that I knew I was saved, I began to try to get everybody else converted. When I had revival in my own life, the college tutors tried to transfer me into Theology. I was unwilling to do it, because the course was too theoretical for my revival emphasis. I had seen a friend of mine come up to the university full of enthusiasm – he got so full of theory and politics, that he left an atheist!

I certainly had gone through a 'crisis of faith' – in the bible and in the relevance of the study I was doing. Academic history did not seem to be taking me anywhere. I thought medicine – particularly with my recently-converted friend – was a much more practical subject. But they said to me, "No, you've got your scholarship in History, you must stick to this. What you've begun you must finish."

This was a valuable lesson in discipline. In fact, my secular tutor in history said, "You're a religious man, you ought to know, 'He that putteth his hand to the plough and looketh back is not fit for the Kingdom of Heaven.'" **(Luke 9:62)** Was it God speaking through an unconverted person?

Like the early Methodists with Charles Wesley, I owe Oxford a lot in self-discipline, which is essential to a teaching ministry, particularly in a prophetic and miracle age. Through the help of another scholar, I also came to accept the bible as the Word of God, (**2 Timothy 3:16**), which enlarged my submission to His Word and made my later faith possible. I decided I would do extra studies in addition to the degree course in the second year.

In the Preliminary Exams, I was awarded a Distinction. In the second year there are no public exams. The third year at Oxford is the big Final Honours examination. The second year, I went in for a college prize essay on, 'The Growth of the Church Parish System'. That extended to a hundred pages – I remember having to get it typed – and was limited in its conclusions, for a Prize Essay specification. I added about twenty-eight appendices on church ornaments, architecture, the church as the founder of the teaching system in the schools, and the church tithing system – which led to rates; and went right through all history from the very beginning of time in all those subjects.

This placed me in a special position to speak with authority on the development of Church growth and the pit-falls of habit replacing enthusiasm. Charles Wesley, and others who wanted to have revival, found that they weren't allowed to speak outside their parish, which had a constricting influence. America, however, came under the Bishop of London. This country had to find a whole new, more mobile organisation. The rigid parish structure could not contain the new wine. I discovered that the 'sawdust trail' of preaching was birthed out of this, and led to a more mobile society, with a whole new emphasis on feeling the power of God.

At that time I had access to the Bodleian General Library at Oxford – which has a copy of every single book published. How invaluable this was for a rounded view of the subject I was studying. There are certain opportunities we need to take, as they may never recur. Today, I remain grateful for this student experience.

I was also introduced to other prize studies for the University. I wrote on a religious subject, 'Fenelon – Archbishop of Cumbrae.' That essay, as well as the other one, introduced me to new visions. Fenelon's friend was Madame Guyon, who had dreams and supernatural visitations. She was a person persecuted by the Church, who went into what they called 'Quietism' – a form of Quakerism – waiting on the Spirit.

I was becoming encouraged by my studies to seek the Spirit's move. At this time I also had a real battle in accepting the fact that the Lord Jesus had died for my sins on the Cross, and that my debt was fully paid by Him. I wanted so much to earn God's love – either by good deeds or by church-going. I owe a great deal to Michael Green at Oxford, who lovingly showed me that salvation is a gift of God, **(Ephesians 2:8)**, although it can lead to a life of service. **(Ephesians 2:10)**

It was a real emotional battle to come to terms with God's unconditional love. Somehow, I felt that I had to deserve that love by doing or being somebody worthy. This may well have come from my fractured childhood, where relationships, especially in a boarding school, were not easy. The Lord graciously allowed me to come to terms with His unearned love for me – even as a sinner. This allowed me to see His grace and to extend that same love to others. I believe this to be foundational to what happened later in my life.

This is a very real problem for those who suffer from a parent's death or divorce. I found myself only able to break free from this bondage when I saw the love of Jesus on the Cross, where God was in Christ dying on my behalf. (2 Corinthians 5:19-21) This satisfied at once God's holiness, which must punish sin, and His love, which enabled Him to release me from its penalty. When He said, "It is finished," (John 19:30), there was nothing left for me to do but to accept it. This did not mean, however, that I did not have to extend that same forgiveness to others.

During my time at Oxford, I experienced a reconciliation within my own family. I had a feeling that I should make it up with my Aunt Margaret, who had seen my father through college – although my mother felt threatened by her. I wrote a letter to her apologising for my attitude to her, we met, and she remarked that a poor student like myself could do with a new pair of shoes, and promptly went out and got me a pair!

On the University Mission to Mordern which followed, I had the joy of seeing eight people personally receive Christ as Saviour because of my witness. Repentance and reconciliation were shown to me as the basis for true holiness and fruitfulness – and this was the basis also of the later Irish revival. By now I was going regularly to the Scripture Union meetings, and I began to read of revival – about the great 1945 revival with Duncan Campbell, in Barvas, in the Hebrides. I learned also about prayer and fasting as vital for every new move of God.

Because I now accepted the bible as God's Word, my whole attitude to my career changed. I was led to think about not going to a High Church College, but to an evangelical one. God was graciously leading me onwards. I am not against theological study for professional teachers, but I do not believe this is the most important study for everyone in the church. I have been through theological college, deliberately choosing an evangelical one, although it wasn't dramatically academic. In fact, the Principal, Llewellyn Roberts, was a very godly man, who had lived for many years in a parish. He was a very prayerful person and he would tell one exactly how the Lord can bless a church.

We had an Irishman who was a very brilliant scholar and teacher in Hebrew. He would preface his lectures on Old Testament Hebrew with, "This is what the books say – but this is what the Hebrew says!" This was a wonderful introduction to the teaching of 'saints and scholars', which has given Ireland a unique place in the Christian church.

At this time, my mother returned from Canada, where she had left my brother, moving down to Newtown Poppleford, near Sidmouth, in order to be near me at the culmination of my studies towards a Church career – but God had other plans!

We had revival prayer meetings at Theological College at five o'clock in the morning – about three attended! I was praying one morning with Brian Hurd – who later became Archbishop Hurd in Africa – when God spoke to me and gave me this calling, "My sons, do not be negligent now, for the Lord has chosen you to stand before him and serve him, to minister before him and to burn incense." (2 Chronicles 29:11)

It is vital to have a precise divine calling in the ministry – not just the ordination of man. Anytime that I have had a query on my calling, it has been really good to be able to go back to that word from God. I believe you need a call, you need a character, you need a confirmation, and then you have something to stand upon, down the years. Faith needs a personal word from God. **(Romans 10:17)**

While I was witnessing to the college staff, the cook said to me, "You come along and see our Baptist Church." I said, "Are they interested in revival?" "Oh yes!" she said, and that was enough for me. So I went along to see this Baptist man – Robert Rowlands – a big, fat-faced, jolly preacher.

I said, "Robert, see that BMW sitting outside? You shouldn't have a big car like that, with a poor church like this." He graciously replied, "Well, quite honestly, I used to be a BMW executive. If we're going to pray together, we're going to have to get rid of this feeling you have against me."

Then he explained: "Gladys Aylward, a lady who lived by faith, came along, and she just put her hand on my old car, which wouldn't start, and said, 'Lord, give him a good car.' Later, my neighbour said, 'I've sold a lot of houses and I have tithe money. Mr Rowlands, it's painful to see you trying to start that car. Get yourself a decent one.' So I got this one, and because of my former job, I know the worth of the BMW." I felt terribly small, but something broke between us.

Robert and I began to pray, and a lot of folk were saved in his Baptist Church in Bristol. I felt that our reconciliation was a key to this revival. However, before this occasion, God had already begun to challenge my attitudes and thinking. Could He overcome my early fear of poverty, without the security of a professional income?

At my Bristol College, I was challenged through George Mueller's life. He was among the early Plymouth Brethren, and refused to rely on a regular salary, merely leaving a box for gifts at the door of the meeting. He proved that it is possible to trust God and not have a regular income, by sustaining over two thousand orphans by simply praying in their needs each day.

I was challenged in my whole lifestyle. I had gone to an Anglican Bible College expecting a ministry, a settled salary and recognition in the Church of England. God said to me, "I have given you a call to the whole church, and I will give you a salary." This was both a new vision and a new step of faith.

First, He showed me that I could not remain where I was. Through **Hebrews 10:22**, He challenged me in the Anglican doctrine on baptism. "Let us draw near to God with a sincere heart, in full assurance of faith, having our hearts sprinkled to cleanse us from a guilty conscience, and having our bodies washed with pure water." The bible does not teach sprinkling the body – you sprinkle the heart. A few little drops of water on a baby are not going to baptise you – your body has to be washed – and the Greek means a total immersion.

Some people say to me, "I was baptised as a baby," I have to reply, "You weren't – baptism is a total immersion." Also in this verse, it would seem that, before you can get totally immersed, your heart has to be sprinkled – you have to believe on Christ personally, and know a heart change by the blood of Jesus.

Philip dealt this way with the Ethiopian in **Acts 8**, "What doth hinder me to be baptised?" "Do you believe?" he replied. This was not in line with Anglican teaching. God faced me with the issue that, according to the Church of England Prayer Book, I would have to say of babies, "This child is now an inheritor of the Kingdom of God" – knowing that the child had not yet made his or her decision for Christ.

I could not, in conscience, do it. Action followed conviction. I said to the college Principal, "I think I should be baptised as a believer, by total immersion." He said to me, "You realize that if you do that, the church can no longer support you" – the church were paying my fees at a hundred pounds a term. I realized there would be an immediate price to pay, as well as the long term change of career.

I remember going home, and telling my mother, "I'd like to be baptised," and her reply, "Don't you do anything so foolish – you'll catch a chill, and die of pneumonia in two days." I thought, "That's not very encouraging!" She had been baptised as a believer, herself, but she had a human and motherly concern.

I went to the local Baptist minister and said, "I'd like to be baptised." He said, "I wish I could oblige you, because you're only home for the weekend, but, you see, we haven't opened up this baptistry for two years, so we've never had anybody baptised, and none of the men usually attend the prayer meeting tonight. I'll see what I can do for you, but I can't promise you." It seemed I was on my own. I asked the Lord, and the Lord Jesus said that as He had been with Daniel, he would be with me.

At five o'clock on Sunday morning I got a verse from

Acts 22:16, "What are you waiting for? Arise and get baptised, calling on the name of the Lord." I tucked away my swimming trunks and my towel, walked up to the church and the pastor met me at the door saying, "An amazing thing – sixteen men came to the prayer meeting last night, so we've opened up the baptistry, and I thought you should know." I said, "God told me at five o'clock this morning, and I've come prepared" – and I was water baptised.

When I went back to Theological College, they said, "That's your last term!" Then I found a letter addressed to me, and inside was one hundred pounds – an anonymous gift covering my entire fees! The bible says, "If you seek first the Kingdom of God and his righteousness, all these things will be added." **(Matthew 6:33)** There were some more surprises in store – even greater than the money miracle – as I soon found out.

4

Waiting on Tables and the Holy Spirit

I began to attend the evangelical church, where I had been baptised, at Sidmouth. They then warned me, "There are some mad people down the road, called 'Pentecostals'." In a small town like Sidmouth, everybody knew everybody else. I had already become interested in the Holy Spirit and revival, so I went along to their meetings. I was then waiting on tables in a local hotel, because I couldn't continue in my training, but had to earn for my mother, who was a widow.

Among these Pentecostals, I heard of a 'baptism in the Spirit' and I became hungry for this further experience, evidenced by speaking in tongues. (**Acts 10:44-46**)

At that time I remember going to every single meeting for six months and getting terribly discouraged. Everyone else was blessed – except me. The bible actually talks in terms of a man seeking a gift to help a friend. **(Luke 11:10)** I think that many people seeking baptism in the Spirit need to remember that it is a definite blessing based on giving, and not just receiving. It is not simply in order to do something for ourselves, it is meant to be a means of blessing others, whom we lack the power to help without it.

On the same night on which they gave me robes for my Degree, I went to the Oxford Pentecostal Church. I wanted the real white fire of the Holy Ghost – not the white rabbit fur on my gown. I kept them very late at the prayer meeting, until, at two o'clock in the morning, one of them received a prophecy, "Stop looking to get, and start seeking to give." And then they gave me this verse, **(Luke 11:10)**, "Everyone who asks, receives; he who seeks, finds; to him who knocks, the door will be opened."

Now look at that – "ask, seek, knock, everyone ..." These are repetition words, not a single action, for all seekers. People say, "Oh, I came once for the baptism and it never happened." They give up so easily. This is not what Jesus taught here.

I remember speaking and praying with one such person in Lisnaskea Hall – I said, "Brother, have you been seeking the baptism, here in Co. Fermanagh, N. Ireland?"

He said, "Boy, have I been seeking the baptism! I haven't missed a meeting in the Pentecostal church for the last eleven years."

"And what has the pastor told you?" I asked.

He said, "I have been told that I'm not emotionally able to take the baptism, because I'm not free to pray aloud."

I said, "Well, brother, what does the bible say?"

He read out aloud, "Everyone that asks, receives." **(Luke 11:10)**

"What's the problem?" I said.

He said, "I'm afraid. Maybe I will get something strange or bad."

I told him, "Now look at verses **11-13**, 'What father among you, if his son asks for a fish, will instead of a fish give him a serpent; or if he asks for an egg, will give him a scorpion? How much more will the heavenly Father give the Holy Spirit to those who ask Him.' You can't get something bad because God's character would not allow it – you're bound to get something good."

He said, "Well then, that's for me – that's for me, now!"

With that, he put up both his hands, started to pray aloud in tongues, and we couldn't get him to speak in English! We had to get a taxi to take him home to Enniskillen, and he couldn't speak English for three days! When you've been seeking the baptism for eleven years, you are apt to enjoy the experience.

At the same time, ministers need to find out the blockages that the people have, and deal with them from the Word of God – by spending quality time with scripture.

At Sidmouth, I was going to every single meeting, seeking the baptism. The Lord saw my hunger and graciously began to talk to me about Him being my Father. Prophecies were given about a future outpouring of power.

These were real personal needs in my life, which had to be addressed – with the impression that I had of having lost so much. One afternoon, I got the key to the local Pentecostal church and I prayed alone with God. I began to ask, "Lord, if you are a covenant-keeping God" – this is how they prayed in the revival in the Hebrides – "you've got to 'pour water on him that is thirsty'. I know I'm not worthy – but I'm very thirsty." (Isaiah 44:3)

That night a 'message in tongues' was given aloud – by a road sweeper, I remember. Then the pastor interpreted, "Thus saith the Lord, I am your Father and your Saviour. I am a covenant-keeping God" – God had come back to me with the words I had said alone in the afternoon – "The power of the Highest shall come upon you, therefore seek ye My face."

So I continued to run to all the Pentecostal meetings – and got nothing. There was a valid reason for this. A problem which I had in my mind, was whether 'tongues' were made up. Then God did another miracle, in Exeter, in Devon, in 1955.

Brother Edgar Parkins had come home from Africa and he prayed for me in Exe Island Assemblies of God church. By this time, everybody was expecting me to go forward every time there was prayer – I did the expected thing, went forward. Suddenly, I heard him speak in fluent Latin, praising the blood of Jesus. When I heard a recognisable language spoken, all my doubts suddenly disappeared. I knew also that Edgar Parkins was actually praising the blood of Jesus Christ, supernaturally, in Latin – and I knew that the Devil does not do homage to the Blood. At that, the power of God hit me and I went between three or four chairs, without hurting myself, onto the ground. Waves of divine power went over me.

That was the beginning of an introduction to some of the supernatural experiences, which have enabled us to

56

survive the years of death and destruction in Ireland. Friends in the Oxford Elim Church had advised me to be more outgoing and giving, rather than just seeking for personal blessing from God. The man in **Luke 11** got what he wanted, because somebody had come to him, and he wanted to serve him – not simply because of his persistence in asking. I was challenged to begin to do the same.

I gave my testimony in Exeter and then, in Tiverton, just a little after that, as Brother Webb, of the Assemblies of God, prayed for me, I began to speak in a few syllables of a new tongue. Is this scriptural or should there be a full flow of immediate language? Many people, like myself, have this problem. In **Isaiah 28:11**, the Lord says, "With stammering lips and another tongue will I speak," and that stammer – "ss ss ss," "d d d d d" – is genuine.

We have three children and when they began to speak, they didn't say, "Daddy, I want a bottle tomorrow morning at six o'clock." They said, "Da da da", "Ma ma ma." And so, like a little child, we begin a new language. "With stammering lips and another tongue" – note the two stages to the experience. Definitely, God is speaking here about tongues – "I will speak to this people."

The lack of fluency in this prayer language became a real stumbling block to me. As I began to get this stammer, I had this thought – and I've prayed for thousands of people for the baptism and the Devil often uses this tactic – "I've made it up!" Sometimes the doubt comes this way – "I've copied it!" Satan did the same with Jesus – after His baptism when the heavens opened and God said, "Thou art my beloved son," (**Matthew 3:17**), the first thing the Devil said was, "<u>If</u> You are the Son of God." (**Matthew 4:6**)

When you've genuinely spoken in tongues, and had a genuine baptism, the devil tries to put doubt into your mind – he even tried it with Christ. Now, brother Webb was very wise, he said, "Keith, it's not the emotion of the meeting, it's supernatural – this is God. If you still think it's emotion, however, go away and begin to do it again – practice the presence of God, pray on your own." I responded next day to this suggestion.

I went to a little Anglican church near Exmouth. When I saw the stained glass windows, I thought, "There's no mad emotion here." I began again to praise. All of a sudden, the window seemed to burst into light, and the Lord came towards me. I found that my syllables became sentences and the sentences became a language. I was speaking in tongues fluently at that stage. I knew I had received a real experience, because, (**John 16:14**), "[The Spirit] will bring glory to me by taking what is mine and making it known to you." He makes the Lord more real. He gives a new vision of Christ.

At the same time, God confirmed that His promises to me were reliable. This was a great help in knowing that the promises of revival – that the Spirit would come upon all His people – are now being fulfilled. (**Joel 2:28** and **Acts 2:17**) Because it took me a long time seeking, I would say to anybody, "Seek, knock, and ask." (**Luke 11:10**)

The Spirit is sometimes received by loving persistence by the seeker, not automatically by his relationship or friendship with the Lord. I had been very discouraged and I did have this intellectual blockage on tongues. God graciously dealt with it by showing me a definite language as I continued to seek Him.

As well as personal commitment and effort, however,

there is a stage of receiving and resting. Like having a natural baby, there comes a stage of relaxing and speaking, in baptism in the Spirit. Co-operate with God by not continuing to use your native tongue. Begin to use your lips to speak out the new words. **(Acts 2:4)** You cannot speak two languages simultaneously. Stop praying in your native tongue. Start using your new syllables – you can start and stop. **(1 Corinthians 14:21)**

Very often since that, when praying with people, I've told them to relax. This has been a key. The more they tense up, the more they speak in their native language, then the less likely they are going to be able to receive the language God has given them.

What is the point of speaking in a prayer language? The Holy Spirit helps us to pray when we don't know what to say. **(Romans 8:26)** And so in my prayer life now, if I don't know how to pray, I'm able to speak in tongues.

Three years ago, Bill Turner and I stood in front of the life-support machine, in the Ulster Hospital, near Belfast, and we saw a lady whose breathing was interrupted. The life-support machine was registering death. What should we pray?

Together, Bill and I prayed in tongues. As we watched, the needle began to move on the machine. Three days later, the lady was out of intensive care, while the nurses could not explain the miracle. She's had a baby since then, and is doing extremely well. Prayer in tongues is powerful – even in the presence of death.

On another occasion I prayed in tongues for a Pentecostal man, who had been smoking sixty cigarettes a day. We sensed how seriously he was sick – the angel of death seemed to be at the bed. As we prayed in tongues, suddenly, the man sat up. The doctor who came in was amazed. The man confessed, "I'm a heavy smoker." The doctor shook his head, "You were a smoker. Your next cigarette is your last!" It is strange how some people ignore their pastors and listen to their doctors!

Tongues has been the key to many of the miracles we have seen. I find there is a time when you don't know how to pray, and God gives you the words and the authority. Does that mean that everyone who speaks in tongues automatically gets power? Many people mistake the experience of praying in tongues for a mature ministry of miracles, but the two are different. I know the bible says, in (**Acts 2:18**), "You will receive the power of the Spirit coming upon you" – but that is not the same as a ministry.

Although we have seen many thousands of people speak in tongues, very few have come into ministry. People have asked why this is so. Come with me to **Luke 6:40** – I want to share this with you.

"A student is not above his teacher, but everyone who is fully trained will be like his teacher." The King James Version says, "... will be perfect as his teacher." You cannot improve on the Lord Jesus Christ, but you can be like Him.

What we're talking about here is the ministry of Jesus. He had the Spirit, with water baptism and the opening up of heaven, but then something followed – He fasted for forty days. You cannot get His ministry any easier way. Only when Jesus had bound the Devil in the desert, did he come out to a period of ministry. Many Pentecostal people have had the ability of a prayer language without the ministry. They have never taken the time to bind the Devil in their life, or in the lives of others.

I started a fast of over thirty-five days, soon after my baptism in the Spirit – following fasts of shorter periods of time. During my fast, the Devil appeared to me on the thirty-second night and a tremendous battle took place. He offered me human recognition and wealth, but I declared my intention of following Jesus into poverty and dishonour, if only I could live and die in His Kingdom.

I asked God then to allow me the use of all the Gifts of the Spirit, and a praying sister visited me with the promise – since fulfilled – that this would happen, but only when they could be used to help others. Service and power can never be separated in the Kingdom. Meanwhile, there were other things that God was trying to show me, about the outworking of a church totally empowered by the Spirit. That was soon to happen to me.

5

Chard and Revival

At first I made the mistake of trying to get all the gifts of the Spirit – wisdom, knowledge, faith, healing, working of miracles, prophecy, discernment of spirits, tongues and interpretation of tongues. (**1 Corinthians 12:8-10**) The Lord actually gives them in one total package at the baptism, (**John 3:34**), when the Spirit gets you.

I was blessed with the support of a godly church at South Chard, where a lady explained to me that, when you're filled with the Holy Spirit, you not only speak in tongues, but all the gifts of the Spirit become yours. You get everything when you get baptised, because the Spirit gets you. The use of these gifts occurs only when you need them, to pass on to somebody else. I thank God now for this revelation and teaching. At Chard, God brought me into a church which was bible-based and sustained by God. I remember the elder, brother Sid, almost had a nervous breakdown, because he was trying to carry the church and the ministry alone.

He was also constructing houses on a contract as a builder. The church business was beginning to drag him down. One night, he went to bed, feeling quite sick, and the Lord gave him this promise, **Matthew 16:18**, "I will build my church, and the gates of Hell will not prevail against it." God gave him a promise that if he would just relax, and commit the church to Him, God would do it. He got up from his bed at once, totally healed.

From his Brethren viewpoint, he could understand the ministry of the whole Body. He opened the sharing to the whole church, so that the Holy Ghost was free to move, and the platform was open for anyone anointed of the Spirit to speak. This was a bold new concept to Pentecostals.

It was at this time that a Pentecostal evangelist was invited, who was appalled to discover that there had been no proper ordination of elders. Three of us were chosen – Sid himself, with a signal box man and I, to help him. As the burden became heavier, I realised the importance of delegation. From this evangelist, I also had some contact with Ireland, and learnt to view the church as a missionary centre. My own calling, also, was to travel.

At this time I met another brother, a prophet, in a group just outside Chard, who had also developed prayer meetings for revival. There was a girl there, called Rose, who used to experience quite an unusual miracle of the Spirit, new at that time – of being physically moved a number of miles, under the power of the Holy Spirit. This prophet gave me a word, "You will go and sow God's Word."

In this group, I saw how God could use ordinary people in a deep prophetic way, which fulfilled the bible ideal of a church dependant upon supernatural ministry, and not limited by education or social standing. This was a practical fulfilment of the vision I had caught from George Mueller, and the earlier Plymouth Brethren movement, from which these people had come.

In Chard, we held early morning prayer meetings and some fasting for several days. There was a solid prayer background to the beginning of the work. We had then about twenty or thirty people, but the numbers grew dramatically afterwards, with other ministries coming in. Later, we became an evangelistic centre for the area.

Many people joined, who wanted to go deeper with God and be free in the Spirit to sing and dance. They found that Holy Ghost vision always brings a release. Revival also sparks off a real missionary effort – a concern for souls on a wider basis – as well as warming up Christians. Once God has got His own people right, the unconverted begin to come to Christ.

Chard became a centre for a whole new level of missionary activity. Exciting things began to happen. In the early days of an outpouring of the Spirit, the Holy Ghost was allowed to take charge of the meeting – that was the emphasis. There was also a Brethren emphasis on the scripture. That was a good foundation for a balanced ministry.

Through Chard, I met Arthur Wallis, who was a great man of prayer. He had a lot of contact with the Ward family, who lived near me at the time. They spent time in prayer, and sometimes sister Ward would describe events at a distance. Christ in her would enter into what was happening miles away.

For example, there was a man in Africa, who was being beaten, and she could actually feel the beatings. With this heavy prayer identification, she was able to pray him through a crisis. Some of these incidents Arthur recorded later in the final chapter of his book, 'In the Day of Thy Power'.

Later, I met others, who could actually feel sickness or even demon power affecting people in their own bodies, and learnt what it is to have the indwelling Christ ministering deeply in prayer for healing and deliverance. I have seen miraculous results from such praying.

God has shown me, however, that you don't compare yourself with anyone else – what we are, we are by the grace of God. I have never felt inferior because of the lack of such experiences personally. We're placed in the church by Jesus Christ, we don't compare with each other. We move forward in God, who has a personal calling for each individual – often with different physical manifestations. I am content to be myself in God, and yet allow the viability of others who are serving Him in different ways. This is a real secret of rest and progress at the same time.

We had just a few members at South Chard in those days. As we fasted and prayed and committed the church to Jesus, the numbers grew rapidly – so God fulfilled His promise to uncle Sid to build the church, when He healed him previously. Meanwhile, God began to use me in travelling.

One of the dangers of a successful small group, is spiritual development without a concern for the lost. This should be a constant focus for action by leadership. I remember particularly we went to a convention in Kent. In the afternoon, I could see the evangelist was a good preacher, but I couldn't understand why there was no blessing. So instead of having tea, afterwards I set aside a time for prayer – I was learning to fast at that time. An angel appeared and I actually saw his feet.

I began to pray urgently and came against what the enemy was doing in the convention. Now the preacher was the same that night, but there was a difference – forty-one people were saved in that meeting, as a result of my laying hold of God in prayer between the meetings. Ministry in meetings is very dependant on what happens before they start. God prepared me, through fasting, to see a bigger vision of victory over Satan, the 'strong man', before we would see the captives set free.

However, before these events in Chard, God had shown me that I should earn a living – and here there were some new lessons in store.

6

Teaching and Still Learning

About a year before this, the Lord had impressed on me that I should use my degree to teach in school, so I had applied for a teaching job with an agency. I was hired for temporary duty at a private boarding school near Camberley, in Surrey, England. It was a special school for children who had separated parents, or a father or mother that had died.

When I arrived at the school chapel and saw the candles on the altar, the celebration of Prayer Book services, I thought, "Oh dear. What am I meant to be doing here? I'm back in the High Church atmosphere I was in before." They told me that I was chosen to be temporary Chaplain, but I could only stay a year because I wasn't properly ordained.

While I was wondering whether I was in the right

place for the Spirit to move, the Headmaster came to me and said, "I want you to read the lesson." So I opened up the bible and the passage they gave me was **Jeremiah 1:7 (KJV)**, "The Lord said, do not say 'I am only a child', you must go to everyone I send you to" – so I didn't have much option!

The next verse added, "Do not be afraid of them, for I am with you and will rescue you, saith the Lord." I began to preach the gospel – that God could become our Father through a New Birth – in my Divinity classes. My impression was that this was totally new to most of the boys.

There was another keen Christian member of staff, a Baptist man, who was teaching science at that time. We became a team to help the students. I heard of a 'mad evangelist' in the area, who was holding house meetings, and teaching a series on the Song of Solomon. I went along to this house meeting – and there was Roger Forster taking house meetings as a Brethren evangelist. This was the beginning of a friendship which has deepened through the years in a parallel ministry in the Lord.

Meanwhile, something new was happening at the school. A young lad came to me and said, "I made a previous decision to ask the Lord into my life. I have wandered for some years, but I want to come back to Jesus Christ." That night he made a decision for the Lord. His friend, who was involved in criminal activities, ignored him, and soon after was arrested by the police. The first young boy could have gone the same way. Instead, he went and told his friends, and during the next seven days, twenty-eight boys in that school were wonderfully touched and changed by the grace of God. A whole new atmosphere of love pervaded many lonely lives.

When it was time for me to leave, the headmaster told me, "By the way, I sent for you because I'm also 'born-again' and I wanted a gospel witness in the school. The governors are so pleased with you, they're going to give you four hundred pounds as a bonus." I left the school marvelling at the way God had kept His promise to me, from Jeremiah, on the first day.

Results do not always come so quickly, when a promise is given by God, but it always pays not to be discouraged by appearances, and to believe Him for a miracle. Some results will only be apparent at the end of time, or even in eternity, but it does show that we need to start the day with the Word of God, if something lasting is to be accomplished. The Lord Jesus Himself obviously did so, "Very early in the morning, while it was still dark, Jesus got up, left the house and went off to a solitary place, where he prayed." (Mark 1:35 NIV) God needs to speak, even during apparent success, to move you on to something better of His choice.

Between revivals, there is also a need for physical rest and relaxation. After teaching at that school for a year, I went back to waiting at tables for a period. I then became very aware that God had another job for me. Suddenly, I received a letter from a headmaster, who had a school in Ireland, near Enniskillen. Now, I'd never been in Ireland before. I was under the impression that people there kept pigs in their cottages, etc., and were generally very backward – I could not have been further from the truth!

Yet I felt God was leading. The Headmaster, a jolly man with a large smile, came to England to interview me. He said that they needed a divinity teacher as their previous teacher had been suddenly appointed to a university. He decided to hire me on the spot, and said, "Right, that's it. Here is your fare to come over and a five pound note. You start in a month and you've got to organize the whole syllabus, and a prize course for the students as well."

When I arrived in Enniskillen, I found that many of the boys had fathers who were professional Ministers, and yet their children did not always have personal relationships with the Lord Jesus. Each new generation has to find God personally.

I felt that I needed fellowship to help me in this situation. I asked if there was a Pentecostal man who spoke in tongues. I was told, "Yes, there's a working class man, a Jimmy Kenney who mends shoes. He's got a motorbike, and if you want any fellowship, maybe he will give you a lift." I ventured, "Well, are there any open-airs?" "Yes, there's a Salvation Army open air, where Major Hazard shouts, 'Hallelujah,' with a local doctor." So I joined the doctor and shouted, "Hallelujah." Dr Theo Warmington became a firm friend and colleague in Fermanagh.

I began to pray and fast for revival, as in the previous school. God brought in a like-minded mathematics master and a house mistress, who later became his wife. Both of them were previously converted to Christ, together with another junior teacher. I began to teach a definite experience of salvation and encouraged the children to read the bible, giving them enthusiasm for the bible, which they seemed to lack before this. It used to be just one of those subjects which was compulsory twice a week, and was about as inviting as a nasty medicine!

I took my work quite seriously, and I think the Headmaster was glad that I did. He gave me a lot of support while I was there. For six months we were just fasting and praying, and importing Christian books into the library – waiting on the Spirit to move. It takes a long time to build unseen foundations for something that will last. I became discouraged, because nothing much was happening, but, about half-term, God gave me a promise in my morning quiet time.

The promise He gave me was in **Jonah 4:10,11.** The Lord said, "You have been concerned about this vine, though you did not tend it or make it grow. It sprang up overnight and died overnight. ... But Nineveh has more than a hundred and twenty thousand people, who cannot tell their right hand from their left, and many cattle as well. Should I not be concerned about that great city?" Immediately, God said, "I am concerned about these children. I am going to save these children. What are you going to do about it?"

There is a time to pray and a time to act. I said, "Well, Lord, I could believe that You're going to change some boys next week." Again, the Lord said, "What are you going to do about it?" Sometimes the Lord asks a question, "Why do you want gifts of knowledge – is it just curiosity or do you want to change your life? Is this to gain personal attention or do you want to help somebody?" God expects an honest answer. He does not give gifts without motivation. **(1 John 3:20,21)**

I said, "Well, Lord, I believe we'll have twelve saved next week." The Lord said "Well, are you prepared to look after them?" I said, "What do you mean Lord?" "Well, do you have booklets to give them? Can you do the follow-up?" I said, "I haven't." He said, "You'd better get hold of some books, because I am going to work." I accepted this challenge that morning.

I wrote to the Scripture Gift Mission – my first contact with Elsie – and I received twelve emphasized Gospels of St. John, with decision forms in the back. I thought this was big faith – twelve decisions in one term. Do you know, the day the books arrived, six kids gave their hearts to the Lord? Then the next class down was taught by a lady who was a Christian. In her class, the first six kids led another six to the Lord. They explained to her, "Mr. Gerner's boys acted as our priests" – they only knew these sort of terms – "They led us to Jesus. Now how do we get hold of the books?"

They told all their brothers in the higher part of the school, so in the first month I had twenty-four decisions for Christ – and not enough books! When you mean business, I have found that "He is able to do abundantly above all that you ask or think." **(Ephesians 3:20,21)** The enthusiasm was such, that it interfered with some of the running of the school. Suddenly I was in difficulty – I was requested not to see the boys privately. It didn't matter, because the boys led each other to Jesus. One boy led eleven souls to Jesus the first week he got saved! He was offered a place on the school tennis team, but when he was told they played matches on a Sunday, he said, "That's me out, I'm a Christian." There was a tremendous sense of the presence of God. They even prayed for each other in the sanatorium and the sick were healed.

Meanwhile, I continued to pray night and day for these new converts. I was stopped a couple of times by the British Army, coming home from a prayer time. They asked, "Where have you been?" "I've been to Brookeborough, where Sergeant Cross is praying for a revival." The soldiers thought I was crazy, but God was in it. While we were praying the following Saturday at Brookeborough, there was a knock on the door, and there stood some of my sixth formers, "Please, sir, we want to get God in our lives." Revival was very real.

As this move of God peaked, the Lord again spoke to me, that I should move on. It was obvious to me that that chapter was closing, so I handed over the pastoral care of the boys to other Christian teachers and went home to England. A deep impression was left in my life however, of the need in rural Ireland. This has never left me over the years.

While I was at the school, I noticed that in the whole of Co. Fermanagh there were only a few Pentecostal people – just a small Elim Church. In the city of Belfast there were fourteen Pentecostal churches in one mile!

In the south of Ireland, as well as in the west of Ireland, there were many areas with only a handful of people who knew the experience of the outpoured Holy Spirit in Pentecostal power. Sometimes through work, God takes you to a place that is going to be your missionary calling. Vision can be born of such a simple work experience. Although I went home to England, to look after my widowed mother, the Lord challenged me with a concern for Ireland.

It was after this, at Chard, that the Lord showed me the development of body ministry, which I detailed in the last chapter.

Pastor Fitzgerald was a visiting Irish evangelist, with his wife, who came from Plymouth, Devon. Because he was from Ireland, there were people coming from Ireland to his church. He greatly helped me into a new use of the Gifts of the Spirit in my life, and asked if I would come to a convention in Plymouth and seek God about missionary work in Ireland. God then challenged me that, if I was to go to Ireland, I might have to leave my mother, who was a widow. Would He be supreme in my life?

I knew that my mother had relatives in Canada and that she could go there, but I believe the call of God should not excuse our family responsibility. Then God spoke again to me through a prophet, "The one that you love will be with you in the work." He challenged me, "Do you love your mother more than Me?" I was confused by this word, because I thought, "the one that you love" must be my mother – and yet the Lord was asking me to leave her. You sometimes try to work out prophecies with your own mind, instead of letting the Lord work it out. Prophecies go beyond natural interpretation. Actually, I would later love and marry Elsie, who would be with me in the work.

My mother left shortly after for Canada, and I went to the Plymouth Brethren Church. I read a passage in Isaiah, telling me that a new ministry had begun for me. **(Isaiah 14:1-2)**

He gave me a calling to Ireland. How would I get

76

there? God woke me up one morning and said, "The ones from across the sea will carry you." Then a car arrived over from Belfast, with an Englishman, and others from the Shankill Road. One man from Belfast had fallen sick, though, so there was a space in the car going back to Northern Ireland. They offered me the spare place – which was all very well until we reached Liverpool docks – I had no money for the boat ticket!

By this stage, Pastor Rowlands was the local pastor in Liverpool, and I thought maybe he could give me some money, so I went to see him – but he was out. I arrived at the boat – still without a ticket, or even the money for the ticket.

When I stood at the ferry and said, "Lord, You'll have to undertake soon," one of the men travelling in the car, who didn't know my circumstances, said, "You need a ticket to Ireland, here's some money," and gave it to me. Sometimes God only undertakes at the last minute. I said to the Englishman, "I need to go to Ireland, I've had contacts there before," and I told him about Fermanagh.

He replied , "I tell you what, God has told me that I'm to look after you."

I said, "Well, where's your home?"

He laughed , "I haven't got one. I've got a wife and three kids and no money, no home – but I am still taking you with me!"

I prayed about this, and the Lord gave me a promise, **(Philippians 4:19)**, "And my God will meet all your needs, according to his glorious riches in Christ Jesus." This was something this Englishman firmly believed in, and was living out, in his own circumstances. We crossed the Irish Sea on the ferry together.

On arrival we began to witness to a person in Belfast, who said, "We have a house in Bangor," and they let us live in the house. We laid the table with knives, forks and spoons and prayed, "For what we are about to receive, may the Lord make us truly thankful" – we hadn't got even a penny! However, a lady came in and gave us money, so we went to buy fish suppers that night. You know how to get to the top of a food line, don't you? You start to give out gospel tracts, everyone wants to get rid of you, and you get right to the front of the line!

What about breakfast? It was now quite late in the day, and also early closing day in Bangor, so although we had money for groceries, the shops were closed. We went across to a grocery shop and knocked. The man answered the door, and said he had been kept there all day because he had a puncture.

Although he could supply us with the groceries, we still needed milk. He volunteered, "I'm sure the man who sells milk is away by now." When we went to get the milk, again the place was closed. But when we knocked, the man who came to the door said he had been kept there all day. He'd sold all the milk he had, though, but when he went into the fridge he came back with two pints labelled 'Friday' – the next day's milk!

He said "Where have these come from? The delivery hasn't come."

"Oh," I said, "come from heaven, probably. How much money do you want?"

"I don't want any money – get out of here." he replied. God can come so close, it becomes uncomfortable. Not everyone wants Him alongside.

Just before Christmas, 1960, we came to Enniskillen,

78

in faith that the Lord would provide us with a hall where we could hold meetings. After some personal witnessing, my new English friend was led to contact the British Legion there, and they immediately arranged for us to use their hall – with its chairs, lighting, heating and piano – all free of charge. Furthermore, we were able to use it to have a breaking of bread and a whole day of prayer on Sundays.

These Sunday services saw increasing attendance and blessing. We came to the decision that, instead of doing a great deal of advertising, we should spend our time in prayer that the Father would send in the people of His choice for one week.

During that week, attendance of those interested mounted rapidly. In 1961 we had the joy of seeing the Lord moving both south and north of the border here. We visited both Bundoran and Sligo in the Republic. In Sligo we were favoured with a sunny day and held an 'open-air' at Rosses Point – right on the Atlantic coast of the Republic – where we had hardly begun to preach before the heckling started.

On hearing my testimony to real deliverance through Christ, however, one of the leading hecklers acknowledged, "You cannot argue with a true experience of the Lord." An ounce of experience can be worth a ton of argument. Our contact with the south of Ireland had begun – though dangerously.

7

Teamwork and Marriage

Elsie now adds her own testimony:

"When Keith was working at Portora Royal School, he contacted the Scripture Gift Mission, listing bible texts that he wanted for the boys. My boss, the secretary of the Belfast branch, couldn't make 'head nor tail' of this man and what he wanted. As he was going to Dublin, he told me that he would go via Enniskillen and call in to see Keith Gerner. There, he told Keith to write to me, because he was going to be away for a week or two. So from then, Keith always wrote to me at the office.

"At that time he put a scripture message at the bottom of any letters he wrote. This time he used the verse, 'You have not chosen me, but I have chosen you.' **(John 15:16)** I had a good laugh at that. I said to the office staff, 'Wait till you hear this girls, I've got my proposal at long last.' They used to tease me about Keith in the office, and I referred to him as 'my boyfriend'.

"At this stage I had never met 'Mr Gerner', knew nothing of his age or whether he was married already, and I was not really all that seriously interested. While all the boys were being saved at the school near Enniskillen, they began an intensified study of scripture. One boy got through the whole bible in three months. It was unbelievable the amount of work that I had to do, giving YSL – Young Sowers' League – awards.

"After this time Keith had left the school, and was travelling around. He had got the boys to be 'lone searchers' – doing bible study, and sending answers to me, which I marked. It got to be, then, that my mail was bigger than that of my boss, Mr. Hinds, and he got a bit upset about it – understandably. He wanted to open my letters. I said, 'You can open my mail, sure I don't mind, so long as you make sure you give it back to me straight away, because I want to answer the children at once.' I didn't want the letters lying at the bottom of the basket for weeks, when I knew the boys were anxious for a reply.

"I went away on holiday, and they told me Keith had been in the office, looking for me everywhere – in all the cupboards! It was all just in fun. Then they said that he was coming back, and I was so embarrassed at the thought of it, because they kept threatening, 'Next time he comes back, we're going to make you blush.'

"I rearranged all the office furniture so that if he came in, I would be sitting with my back to the door and wouldn't see him. I was petrified – every time the door opened, I just froze. He came in to see my boss one day, and my boss called me into the office to meet him – I was so embarrassed, because I knew what was going on in the outer office. He introduced me to Keith, and I got out of the office again, somehow. Before I met him, as already stated, I didn't know whether he was an old man, or married, so it was absolutely ridiculous to joke about him.

"Some time later, my boss called me into the office, to show me a slide he had taken. He said, 'There's somebody in that picture that you know.' I spotted Keith right away, but I was getting redder and redder, so I kept the slide up to my eye and said, 'Oh yes, there's Dr. Warmington' and then, when I'd cooled down a wee bit, I added, 'and there's Mr. Gerner.' We had been writing to each other – purely business of course. Then Keith would call in, and he had nothing particularly in mind – he would go, 'Emmm ... ahh' – he didn't really want anything, he just sort of hung around.

"One day he was coming up to the office to see me, and he met my boss going out. Usually Keith's shirt collar was looking up at him, but on this occasion he came in with hair all Brylcreemed, and his collar straight down – really looking very smart – and I thought, 'Aah. I've had it!' I really felt at that stage that something had happened.

"So then he wrote to me. I had told him that I had a doll, which I used to make dresses for – for my sister, Hazel. I had a lot of clothes for it, and I offered to give it to the daughter of the house, where Keith was living at the time. He wrote back and said that if I mentioned any time, any place, he would meet me to get the doll. I thought, 'No, I'm not falling for that one.' I wrote back, 'It's in the office anytime you want to call to collect it.' If I'd been running after him, or anything, that would have been a wonderful opportunity, but I wasn't having

83

any of it. There were different opportunities like that, but I ran in the opposite direction!

Keith adds:

I was undergoing a similar teasing process from my friends, when I came back to Ireland for mission work, as I described in the last chapter. Marriage, however, I knew to be a serious step. The bible has strong teaching on it. (2 Corinthians 6:14) Being unequally yoked to an unbeliever is clearly taught as wrong, but you should not marry just any believer. You've got to be equally yoked to someone who has the same calling and the same priorities. With our marriage, particularly with the years ahead, the tests and the ups and downs, we've always been able to go back to a direct word from God.

Firstly, we had a joint priority. Secondly we could say, "God said this ...," and therefore we are joined in a definite way with God. I think that has been a great help. Couples should get a definite word from the Lord, rather than just running after any partner who is a Christian.

In Elsie's life there was a moment of re-dedication just before we met, and a desire to really serve the Lord. Elsie received a letter, "If you think more people can be blessed through our remaining single, then Amen, Elsie" – we were already individually serving the Lord – "If not, it's better that we work together."

There have been situations, like taking on settled pastoring work, where Elsie's whole gifting as a wife and mother was important, but her musical gifting was essential to our mobile mission work. The fact of having the family tie was also important for me – never having had a father or family. She was able to have an input to my loneliness from my own background, because she came from a good, solid Christian home. Her mother was very prayerful for her daughters – parents do have something to do with relationships, in the way that they give example and the way that they pray.

Leadership is linked to those who are living the Christian life in family. (1 Timothy 3:4-5) He must manage his own family well and see that his children obey him with proper respect. If anyone does not know how to manage his own family, how can he take care of God's church? I know this has been taken to excess – a friend of mine actually resigned his pastorate when his adult son divorced – and I do believe there has to come a time when the children have to be responsible for themselves.

At the same time, if you go into a home and the children are not in order, the bible suggests that the head of that home is not fit for church leadership. The church is meant to be a family and therefore all experience of fatherhood and the family is equally as important as academic qualifications.

When my English friend and I had travelled in Scotland and around the country – particularly in the campaign work – I began to feel that new churches should be set up, for instance in Cullen, where we had twenty-eight saved. But when I asked who would look after the church, nobody volunteered. My English friend turned to me and said, "Keith, I think you'll have to look after these converts." Now, because I believe a pastor should be married, I thought that, if I was going to be a pastor, I would need a partner in the work.

At this time, Elsie was seeking whether we could work for the Lord together and she went to a meeting and was given **1 Samuel 17:8**, "Give me a man that we might fight together!" – and Elsie and I began to fight for the Lord jointly in our marriage.

Elsie also had a separate call – and in an audible divine voice – giving her direction to read scripture: (**Micah 4:10**), "Writhe in agony, O daughter of Zion, like a woman in labour, for now you must leave the city to camp in the open field. You will go to Babylon; there you will be rescued. There the Lord will redeem you out of the hand of your enemies." I think it's very important when you're working in a partnership that both of you get a call.

The same word that God gave us, separately and individually, was, "You must leave this city and camp in the field." I was then living in Twisden's Field. She felt it was right to go to me. **Micah 4** continues, "And you will go to Babylon. And there you will be rescued, and the Lord will redeem you out of the hand of your enemies." Scotland didn't appeal to us very much at that time, so it was like Babylon. Elsie also felt the responsibility of the vision for the period ahead.

I had spoken at the Christmas convention in Belfast, when a lady came crying to the front. She showed me where her husband had put a knife into her arm, and told how she had married this man as a Christian, hoping to lift him from drink and sin. As she confessed to failing to put the Lord first in their relationship, Jesus appeared to us and spoke forgiveness into her life. Next day, while we were walking together, Elsie pointed out to me that I was giving too mu~ch time to her and not witnessing to needy people, as I usually did.

Immediately afterwards, as I went up to a man who

was obviously distressed, he turned out to be the husband of the lady for whom we had prayed the night before. He confessed his sin, promised restitution and found peace with the Lord – just before our own wedding. We had some wonderful wedding presents from folk, but this was the best. It seemed to seal our union in God – this estranged husband and wife united in Christ, through His grace. At the same time, it was a solemn warning to have God as a priority in our relationship.

8

Outreach in Scotland

We were married on December 30, 1961 – a sunny day after a fortnight of fog and ice. We sailed across to Scotland and, despite threats of blockage by drifting snow, reached the north east coast of Scotland in time for the Sunday evening meeting at Peterhead. Elsie loved the deep snow of the journey – although God did a miracle to get us through.

Our Belfast wedding service had combined a conservative Baptist pastor and a Pentecostal preacher. It contained also a missionary commissioning, but the impact of the dancing Pentecostals in Scotland was a cultural shock. Elsie learned much from the informal days of our honeymoon together in the 'glory meetings', and from the informal and loving home of Pentecostals in Peterhead. We saw how people could be set at ease by being made so welcome in a casual way, and it laid a foundation for our later home in Ulster, where up to two hundred people a week came through our front door.

We had a fulfilment of God's promise in **Micah,** "I will deliver you." A newspaper said they were going to oppose us – a baby had died after its parents refused a blood transfusion for it. The newspaper telephoned saying that it was our fault, and they were sending a reporter to investigate.

The reporter came, and apologized. It proved to have been Jehovah's Witnesses who had told the parents not to have the blood transfusion. Now he asked, "How do you live? Who supports you?"

"Well," I said, "Last week we only had a little bit of money, so we put a shilling in the gas meter and it lasted for five days – until I got worried, and phoned the gas company. A Christian came along to inspect the meter, and found nothing wrong with it, 'God has just done a miracle,' he said, 'you've had five days' gas for a shilling. If you tell the Christians, we're going to be in trouble – so don't spread it around!'" The reporter admitted that he had a Christian background, but had never seen God act in this practical and miraculous way. He went away and gave us a positive write-up.

God was with us in this simple way, to confirm His calling. Covering the whole of Findochty and Port-knockie – in Banffshire, in the north of Scotland – with personal, door-to-door work, we then moved to Portessie, the next town up on the coast. There, in March 1962, we encountered a woman who challenged us with the fact that her sister, a WEC missionary, "took religion too far" – by relying on God to meet every need. "What would happen if every Christian did that?" she asked.

We replied that God would keep them – He fed and kept millions of Israelites in a barren wilderness.

Jesus fed thousands from a few loaves and fishes. Over seven thousand converts of the early church believed God and sold all that they had. (**Acts 2:45 & 4:34**) In fact, Jesus commanded His followers to sell all, (**Luke 12:33**), and work full-time for his Kingdom. "We just obey Him and trust Him to supply each need." This is what C. T. Studd and George Mueller did, while Hudson Taylor applied the same faith when he founded the China Inland Mission. "The Lord Jesus does not change. (**Hebrews 13:8**) Is there anything too hard for the Lord?"

She was shocked: "I would rather earn my own living than depend on God." We asked her if she prayed the Lord's Prayer. When she replied that she did, we asked, "What do you mean by praying, 'Give us this day our daily bread'?"

We had come to talk to her about being saved, and were surprised at the way she supposed every Christian lived by faith like her sister. Anyhow, the Lord led her to ask us for our own testimony, which amazed her, as it did the four reporters whom we had in the next two days, March 7th and 8th.

"We never know where our next penny will come from," I am quoted as saying to each of the reporters – Daily Express newspaper, 9th March 1962 – "but we know that, if we pray for it, we will get enough to keep us." We believed that this interview was a challenge to the whole coast, which was facing a recession in its main industry – fishing. The Lord brought a message of hope.

Living without salary or regular income, the Lord kept us and met our needs – not our greeds. At the same time, we had not lost the vision of a revival outpouring – although we seemed only to be sowing seed all the time, with very little harvest. We began to cultivate praying friends, who would pray for labourers to help us. This led to the formation of a circle of prayer partners. These have been the backbone of our work ever since, and contact with them has been our life-line.

Our friends in Peterhead also began to sense a rising tide of blessing. Already, three young men from the Zion Tabernacle group had volunteered for full-time work in the area. Their first mission, in Newpitsligo, that month was marked by the salvation of four souls and an outstanding miracle of healing on a man who had been sick for over thirty years. In January 1962, we asked our praying friends to intercede for us as we moved up the coast to a new crusade in Buckie Town Hall.

Already our local meetings, in an old church in Cullen, resembled more of a farce than a revival. Certain rowdy young people came to Christ, while others just came to make themselves a nuisance! It was like being in a tremendous spiritual battle – a revival and a riot all in one.

At the same time, three young girls, who were recent converts, took tracts down to the old folks' home and boldly asked the Matron for permission to preach. When they were given it, they spoke with such power that one old lady was in tears – "and so we told her how to get her sins forgiven," was their comment – this from twelve-year olds!

In February, we found ourselves so busy that we took Tuesday and Thursday nights 'off' each week, to spend more time with the Lord – activity was crowding out our more important times of fellowship with the Lord and waiting upon Him. That month, we were also hampered somewhat by the weather, but launched into a literature ministry. Through the kindness of the Scripture Gift Mission, four hundred and fifty copies of the Book of Acts were made available to us for personal distribution in the area.

We also decided to print a tract of our own called, 'Do you want to move a mountain?' – on the theme of **Matthew 17:20** – revealing the Lord Jesus as saviour, healer, baptiser and the One who supplies our every material need. We told nobody of our intended production. On Saturday, 17 February, 1962, we were able to praise the Lord for an anonymous gift that covered the whole cost of printing 10,000 copies.

At that time, we were living in a great deal of poverty, but we had money multiply, food multiply, and we had an unconverted butcher who fed us every weekend, for a pittance, with 'left-over' meat. It was remarkable that God used an unconverted man to supply our needs. Miraculously, his family was saved after we left.

We shared our food also with a Christian next door. It was cheaper to cook on one stove, instead of two. One morning, in front of his family, I came in to take our share of porridge and saw the pot half empty. Thinking they had taken their half, I emptied the pot. When they went to the pot, it was still half full!

We went to take some meetings in Buckie. A local Evangelical minister said, "Yes, I would support you for the gospel – but I'm not so keen on healing."

I thought, "Right, I'll show this fellow how wrong

he is from the bible – give him all the Scriptures," but God told me not to say anything.

One man, called John, came to a meeting on crutches. He put them down when he believed Christ was healing him, and left, walking without the crutches, by the power of God. That Sunday, his minister, amazed at the healing, asked him, "What happened to your crutches?" John said, "God has done a miracle." The minister said, "Come and tell us about it." His minister was the one who was not keen on healing – so I didn't have to do any talking, because God did the talking for me. The Lord did not argue about His ministry or shout at His opposition. (**Matthew 12:19**) He simply carried on the work Father had given Him to do. God then, dealt with the problems.

For the Buckie campaign – 15th-18th of April 1962 – we employed house-to-house personal visits, rather than expensive advertising. This ensured that each person had the gospel, either on the doorstep, through tracts, or by personal letter – even if they never attended the Town Hall meetings. God wants thorough workmanship. We found we could make many really good contacts through visiting. One day my friend, who lived next door to us, was visiting a home and asked a woman if she knew the Lord as her personal Saviour.

"Ask that to me?" she replied, and she laughingly turned to her sister who was visiting her, "He should be asking you that question."

Then her sister said, "But I do know Jesus as my personal Saviour. This is the first time I've told you."

The amazed silence which followed paved the way for my Christian friend to speak to one of the sisters about salvation and the other about following the Lord through water baptism.

Town by town, we witnessed from Buckie right up the coast to Inverness. When we finished taking meetings in that area, we stood on the platform at the railway station, and saw the train coming in – without the money to go. Although my friend next door had loaned me some fare, I felt he could not really afford it. The man in the ticket office put up the little window and said, "Is there a Mr. Gerner here?" "That's me," I said. "Here's the unused portion of the ticket which your friends left behind when they went to Ireland a fortnight ago." Elsie and I caught the train just two minutes later, by the grace of God, and by the supply of His Spirit.

About six months before that time, Len Betts wrote to us to say that he had been told by God to join us. We'd met him before – Len had been with me when I attended Chard. He had been one of the few thousand paratroopers that survived the Battle of Arnhem, before the Lord saved him in a Brethren work near Taunton, Somerset, on the Blackdown Hills. I remember vividly the day he came to our home in Scotland, put his money down and said, "From now on, it's you, me and God. Let's live the New Testament way."

Like the early church, we shared everything – even his motor-bike. He would take us around on his pillion seat, and we spent a lot of time in prayer. Len was well schooled in prayer, and sometimes put me to shame. In Fochabers, for example, we couldn't get a hall because we had no money. "We have not prayed enough about it," announced Len.

Sure enough, as we waited further on God, Len had

a vision of a man standing at a bridge. We went up to the bridge, and standing on it we saw a man in obvious distress. He said, "I've got a problem. I've got two halls booked for Sunday and no preachers." So we got to preach in both his halls and had tea with him between the meetings. Then when Len saw people weren't coming in, he said, "We've got to go out and get them." He approached a group of teenagers, and boldly said to the leader, "You are a coward."

"Who calls me a coward?" roared this big boy, standing well above five-foot Len.

"I do." Len calmly replied, "You used to be a Christian and you didn't have the courage to continue."

Amazingly the big lad hung his head at this Word of Knowledge from the Lord, and Len had the joy of leading two members of the gang to Christ.

There were some Christians in the small fishing village of Findochty, where we lived, yet none of the six or seven Christian groups would fellowship together – a difficult situation to explain to non-Christians. As a result our testimony was weakened.

Our small team of five adults worked together, describing ourselves in one prayer letter as, "Five fingers, one hand – each has a separate testimony to the goodness of the Lord, yet we are united in wishing to be used by the hand of the Lord."

In our team we saw the importance of, "Dwelling in unity, for the Lord to command the blessing." **(Psalm 133:1-3)** It costs much in yielding of self's ways and bringing different temperaments into harmony. We proved however, how worthwhile it is to be, "of one accord in one place," **(Acts 2:1)**, if God were to repeat His

Pentecostal outpouring. Teamwork that exalts Him seems to be critical in these last days before the Lord's return. If the Body is to be built up, there must be unity on the missionary teams and a sense of service to the local church by the five-fold ministries. **(Ephesians 4:11)**

We didn't see any new churches started during our stay in Scotland – we had few people Baptised in the Spirit and, after we went, some of them fell away. This was more a work of sowing the seed and praying against the spiritual strongholds in the area. We went to every town on the coast, really putting out the gospel, giving out tracts and taking small meetings in groups. We usually walked over the ground beforehand, praying.

So we went from Cullen, through every town – Buckie, Elgin – right up to Inverness. When we left, it was with a sense of some disappointment for the effort and prayer expended. God had to teach us later, that what is done in love, and done in Him, is done eternally, no matter what the immediate appearances.

In the 1990s, we went back to that particular part of Scotland – between Buckie and Inverness – which now has Pentecostal churches right up the coast, in every place where we prayed and claimed for God. The folk called us out at the Buckie Pentecostal church, which now numbers three hundred people. The pastor said, "We don't want you to preach, we want to reward you for that year of prayer which you spent in Scotland – you broke through in prayer for revival," and they gave us a generous sum of money. I believe that if you pray over an area, and claim it for God, that will be rewarded.

What then, did we learn in Scotland? Our stay there was a time of great poverty and struggle, when I think

God was asking us what we were in it for. Was it just for an 'easy time', or was it because we loved Him? It was a tremendous time, when God did many miracles of provision and there were over one hundred decisions for God.

We were conscious of the Lord leading us to people in need. Nevertheless, there was a feeling that, once we had distributed tracts around Inverness, we had covered the whole coast. I felt in my spirit a completion of that stage of our vision.

9

Itinerants in Ireland

We knew that we had been called back to Ireland.
Len Betts remained in Scotland for a few months, to look
after the work. He then followed us back to Northern
Ireland. Then he later went to England to help out in a
camp, where he met and married a lady who worked in
Africa. He went out there with her, as a missionary. As
a result of the miracles we had seen in Scotland, Len
faithfully met new challenges in Africa.

There was one time, for instance, when the local witch
doctor had smuggled poison into their hospital, causing
the death of one of their patients. On the way home,
Len and his wife, Ruth, began praying in faith, and as a
result a woman was raised from the dead – he showed
me the photograph. They had been taking her corpse
in a fishing net to his village, when she suddenly sat
up, and walked home – a living testimony to a living
God.

Eventually, Len came back to Ruth's home in Tiverton and looked after their parents and my own mother. Just as Jesus at the cross gave his mother to John, I thank God for Len and Ruth, who looked after mine. We have certainly enjoyed their ongoing faith and fellowship through the years.

When I came back to Northern Ireland, Elsie was pregnant with our first child, Michael, who was born in September 1962. We were living with her parents and, although they were very kind to us, we felt that we needed our own home. Because of our vision to go and sow the Word of God, our first home was mobile.

A brother in the Lord came to us and asked if we would like to tow a caravan in which we could live? He supplied us with this caravan, which was covered with advertising – on one side it read, "What shall I do with Jesus?" (**Matthew 27:22**), and on the other side, "The coming of the Lord draweth nigh." (**James 5:8**) It was soon on the road with the gospel.

We were busy distributing tracts, and doing door-to-door evangelism in Rathcoole – a large housing estate near Belfast. It was an effort, in view of the fact that it included over five thousand separate buildings, some of which were multi-storey flats. This evangelistic outreach was only made possible by some of the young men at Ardoyne Assemblies of God church, who regularly came out with me on Saturday mornings to knock on the doors in all weathers.

So bad were the debt records of those living on this estate that it was nick-named 'Dodge City' by the debt-collectors. It certainly was not one of the richest or most salubrious neighbourhoods to start a work for God.

I was not the leader of the work, but John Stewart, who had initially invited me to take a mission in the area. During 1963, the numbers attending the meetings grew from four to a regular thirty or more, and John was in charge of the follow-up. Although it was a rough area, God saved many precious souls there. A witness for the Lord has continued ever since in that estate.

Meanwhile, I felt myself called not only to work in established meetings, but to launch out into new areas, according to Jesus' commission – "Jerusalem and in all Judea ... and unto the uttermost parts of the earth." **(Acts 1:8)** Obviously, this was followed by an immediate challenge for us to believe God for greater things.

The first need was transport. Belfast was well served by Pentecostal churches, but in May 1963, we felt that we should launch out into rural evangelism. There had not been much in the way of Full Gospel evangelism, particularly in the west of the province. At the time, in the country areas of Northern Ireland, buses did not run so frequently. Although others mention such needs to those who are prayer helpers, we felt led to wait upon the Lord alone.

As a result, we had the joy of getting a 1956 van – with a reconditioned engine from a crash, and with yellow lettered bible texts on three sides – to take us into country areas. This was in the days before it was fashionable to have car window stickers with messages. One side read, "Whosoever shall call on the name of the Lord shall be saved;" the other side declared, "Believe on the Lord Jesus Christ and thou shalt be saved;" and the rear proclaimed, "Jesus said, 'Follow Me.'"

With this vehicle, we were given a trailer. Our caravan, now made road worthy, was our home base for our first outreach to Enniskillen – the area in which I had previously taught, eighty miles from Belfast.

For fourteen weeks we evangelised every major town in Fermanagh. In August 1963, I had an opportunity to give an informal witness to pupils and teachers at my former school, and our first local candidate for baptism took the plunge in the school's open air swimming pool.

That candidate was Johnny, from Enniskillen, an alcoholic who was saved at the local Salvation Army. When his vicar asked him, the following week, how he knew he was saved, he replied respectfully, "Your Reverence, I know I'm saved, for I was there when it happened!" He not only broke free from the taverns, but, after water baptism with us, was able to witness to many people.

A brother in the Lord supplied us with amplifying equipment and we held twenty one open-airs in the first twenty one days of the month, bringing the message of salvation for the first time to many Catholics. Our small team was made up of men whom the Lord had gloriously saved.

The work did not go unchallenged. A doctor was called out to see Johnny because he was supposed to have 'religious mania.' "Where's the patient?" said the medical man as he walked in, "Would you like to sit down and take a smoke? You used to like Players, I remember."

"No, doctor, since I was saved, the desire for them is all gone, glory to God!"

"Well, I've been trying to give them up for years." "Do you know, I think you're the only sensible one in this house?" was the doctor's immediate verdict.

Meanwhile, we needed a more permanent home of our

own, back in Belfast. The greengrocer who supplied Elsie's mother had a sick friend, so we went to pray for him. He was at a hospital in Newtownards, and was actually coughing up blood. He asked me to pray, and as soon as I prayed, the coughing stopped and, after three days, he was allowed to go home. A week later, he was pulling out hedges in his own garden!

The presence of God was very real in that hospital – this healing was divinely accomplished in the medical ward. The impact of this was so great, that the greengrocer acknowledged that he had strayed in his commitment to the Lord. Soon after, he invited us to stay in a small flat above his shop, at the bottom of the Ormeau Road.

We moved in during the autumn of 1963. The flat was situated almost next door to the Belfast gas works, and so was not easy to keep clean. Elsie had to clean the inside of the closed windows daily, as well as the outside – but it was our home and the children loved to play around and to visit the shop downstairs. One of the family even survived a crash through the plate glass door at the bottom! We were grateful to the Lord for His provision. With even the best in-laws, newly-weds enjoy their own home – marriage has to be a 'leaving' and a 'cleaving' in God's pattern.

From our new home, we launched an outreach to Larne, where we distributed five thousand copies of the tract, 'Move a Mountain', and about twenty people came out to the Town Hall meeting. The day was wet and the rotor arm on our van had stuck, so that we had to push the van to a nearby garage. It was Saturday, and the mechanic was out, but a man – who told us that he was a

Communist – lent us his car. "You know where I stand," he said, "but you are the first Christian I have ever met who has sold all and given to the poor. Now that is what I respect." We believe that we were right to give him a testimony of the life of faith, of God answering believing prayer. These were practical terms he could understand.

Today there is a fine church in Larne, planted by young men we trained.

Then, in February 1964, a new event occurred in our family – a baby girl arrived in the form of Heather Joy. "My God shall supply all your need according to his riches in glory, by Christ Jesus." **(Philippians 4:19)** How we proved the power of this promise. With the arrival of Heather Joy, we became in need of a larger caravan for our summer work in the country. Through advertisements, we contacted a brother in the Lord, whose caravan – named 'Everest' – seemed just what was needed. However the quoted price of one hundred and eighty-five pounds seemed far beyond our reach.

At the same time, another brother felt led to make us a fifty pound gift and so we began to pray. Without making an public appeal, but simply believing God, we seemed to be faced by a mountain of need – as high as Everest. Then, almost overnight, the Lord moved on our behalf. The brother who owned the caravan called us of his own accord, to say he would be willing to let us have it for one hundred pounds, 'as unto the Lord', while the other brother doubled his original gift – and so our need was met.

As God had so provided for us, we were able to give away our old caravan, as it stood, to another Christian brother out in full-time labour, so that the work of the

Lord as a whole was doubly blessed. The new home, and new addition to the family, expanded both our horizons and our needs.

Travelling on the mission with us, the children began to learn from us, and we were encouraged by them. In March 1964, I began to appreciate how much God was teaching me about being an earthly father – since I had lacked the experience of having one – and how we should view God in simple trust.

The children grew up fast and they became an object lesson of this simple trust, which we can have in our Father, as children of God. "How much more shall your Heavenly Father give good things to them that ask Him." **(Luke 11:13)** There comes a real rest from this kind of trust in God. **(Hebrews 4:10)**

Shortly after this, we took them to a service in the country and Michael made his way to the pulpit to join me. He was lifted onto the desk, and from there he preached to the people, holding a bible and thumping the desk at the same time. For nineteen months old, his sermon was very good, even if it was given in 'tongues', without interpretation. This was as natural to the children at home, as in the meetings.

As we took Michael up to bed now, he knelt at the cot between us, to say a brief prayer. Although he did not know what it was all about yet, he expected this at night. He knew, too, not to start his meal until I had said grace – which also had to be short, otherwise his 'Amen' came halfway through!

With so many missionaries unable to have their family grow up with them, we feel this was a wonderful gift from the Lord, and one which laid their foundation of their present security and faith in Him. This is one of the great mercies God has afforded us in a ministry which has been extremely mobile.

By 1964, in fact, we had outgrown the little van and were using a larger minibus. This was a year of continuing mission, using the donated vehicle throughout the whole of Northern Ireland – to meetings in Cookstown, Antrim, Armagh, Keady, Dungannon, Antrim again, Whitehead, Muckamore, Ballyclare and Belfast.

By the end of the year, we had records of over one hundred young people and eleven adults having made first time professions of salvation in Christ, fourteen young people and ten adults had returned to the Lord and twenty-eight had been baptised in the Holy Spirit. Obviously the new move to country areas was reaping a spiritual harvest.

1965 was to be a year of continuing outreach – not without its humorous side. While praying with a young man in Dungannon – who received the baptism in the Spirit – I was somewhat shocked to hear the sound of pellets being thrown around the room. To my left, I saw with amazement – green ones, pink ones, blue ones and yellow ones, flying around in all directions. A brother, whose sickness we had prayed for, was emptying his pockets of every pill he could find, in this unorthodox way. His healing was immediate. That is one way of showing your faith that God has healed you, but it was rather an unusual meeting – even by 'Holy Roller' standards.

In this year we covered Dungannon, Whitehead, and Belfast – doing the important work of following up those who had been led to the Lord. (Acts 14:22) God told us then that we had a larger field across the sea. At His call, we gathered our family and, like Abraham, went out to an unknown destination. We crossed over to England, where we saw new miracles.

10

Healing in England

We were called to England, to travel. Literally, we left, not knowing where we were going. Our first stop was Carlisle, where we had an outpouring of the Spirit in the Bible Pattern Church. This new country presented us with a challenge. It is always a thrill to be occupying new territory for God. Carlisle was no exception – six adults accepted the Lord, fourteen were baptised in the Holy Ghost, and others were healed.

A sister with high blood pressure, for whom we prayed, threw away her pills. At her next test, her pressure had dropped by twenty-three points in a week. Before that, she had been ill for months – to God be all the glory!

Our journey to Matlock, which followed, was marked by our radiator boiling on the hills and a near crash with the caravan – what an anti-climax! Elsie was expecting our son Gareth at the time and we certainly had plenty of excitement that night. Our lights failed, and we ignorantly tried to pull our caravan up a very steep hill. We found that the caravan pulled us back, and came to a halt against a wall. The neighbouring people, whom we tried to wake from sleep at midnight, were suspicious of our 'Irish accent', but eventually the local Assemblies of God pastor came to our rescue.

By morning light, we were horrified at the steep drop that lay on the other side of the thin brick wall, against which our caravan was resting. Unknown to us, we had come to country known as the 'English Switzerland' – for its steep hills – for which our old vehicle was not much of a match. At Matlock, the Assemblies of God pastor brightly suggested that we start a new church, at Wirksworth. He gave us, as founder members, his church secretary and his wife. We had to take the initial crusade meetings. The pastor was sure we could succeed – in a small town where three churches had recently closed!

The Lord honoured His word, there were many people saved – and the church secretary and his wife looked after them. There is an Assemblies of God church still in that town today. Once again the vision had proved true. Meanwhile another Assemblies of God opened to us, near the great city of London.

The Watford campaign – 28th August-5th September – had been well prepared by the local Assembly, and almost every night souls were saved. We found ourselves in the police station – because a publican was annoyed about one of our open-airs – but the Lord delivered and the police chief offered an apology.

When a local reporter – an agnostic – came into the meeting, he saw a deaf woman instantly healed, and another Christian, who had grown cold, restored to the

Lord and able to walk without her plaster cast – which she had worn on her back for twenty five years. Slowly, she touched her toes – for the first time in twenty five years! – and was later filled with the Holy Spirit. Those professing salvation included both Catholics and Jews.

We went back to Buxton in October, 1965. Once again the Lord was present in healing power and a woman was healed of a curved spine.

How did non-Christian people view these healings? The answer is interesting. The press estimated:

> *"90 people were healed or touched in the Watford Crusade alone, when a woman walked out of a plaster cast after twenty eight years and touched her toes."*

We have no healing power ourselves. Jesus Christ is the same Healer today. (**Hebrews 13:8**) Frankly, the Watford Observer reporter came as an agnostic. What did he report? Did he believe the story of the lady, claiming to be healed?

His article read,

"Watford Campaign Testimony.

> *While I cannot claim to be completely free from pain, I can touch my toes – for the first time in 25 years – and I am not wearing my jacket, which I was told I must on no account take off. Also, I have not smoked since that night and feel no desire to do so. Mrs. L Snook."*

The Watford Observer reporter, Brian Lecomber, then added,

"Miracle cure of sick?

'Can you hear me?' I whispered. Three feet away from me, the little old lady's face crinkled into a seraphic smile. 'Yes I can hear you clearly,' she replied, 'God has given me back my ears.' The old man, suffering from arthritis, who had been confined to a wheelchair for 6 months, walked out of the church. I spoke to a psychologist on the subject of 'miracles', 'By no means that we know of could a mind cure spinal paralysis after 25 years.'"

Reading of this healing, a man called me to his house for prayer. "I cannot pray for you," I declared. "You have a hard heart."

"No," the man argued, "I have hardened arteries."

"I'm sorry," I replied, "but your heart is hard, and the Lord will not allow me to pray for you."

Outside, the pastor told me that the man was a former member of the congregation, who had kicked over the communion table in temper and was refusing to forgive others in the congregation.

People need to understand that this is Divine healing – not Faith healing – and that God requires confession of sin, **(James 5:14)**, and warns against the wrong attitudes in the Church. **(1 Corinthians 10:1-11)**

One older man, by contrast, was perfectly healed at Buxton, despite the pain he suffered in his joints. His testimony was exciting:

"For weeks I have been unable to walk without pain and discomfort in my left toe joints, and the doctor diagnosed arthritis, but I do praise

the Lord that He has healed me. I went to the front when the appeal was made during the Buxton Divine Healing Campaign and when I left the meeting, I was able to walk without any pain, and my foot is now completely healed."
D. Ford

This testimony, which he wrote for the Buxton Advertiser, was capped by another:

"One lady received healing while sitting in her seat listening to the bible message. On arriving home, she discarded her irons and on Sunday attended the meeting again to relate her wonderful experience. Although her specialist could offer her no further help, Jesus Christ could. An elderly man knelt down without pain for the first time in years."

Philip Hoyle, the reporter at the meetings, was obviously impressed. Apparently, the whole Midlands area was feeling the impact of a new move of the Spirit at the time, and I received a new vision. We needed to train a team for ministry throughout the local area.

At the Wirksworth crusade, a man had told me that there were a hundred Assemblies of God churches in the Nottingham area. Yet they all had to go down to London for training. As a result, Rev. George Yeomans asked me to act as a Principal to train men for ministry locally. That was the burden and vision that brought about the College of Evangelism being set up at Kirkby-in-Ashfield, in January 1966. What a challenge that proved to our trust in God.

When we left full-time evangelistic work in favour

of training others as well, it was in faith that we would continue to have opportunities of daily witnessing, and that the Lord would raise up young people to multiply our ministry. This change gave us the opportunity of proving an 'army of the Lord' for a bigger work, and we found God faithful in times of testing.

A need of a hundred pounds was met by one young person, who was led to save up even before we were needy – "Before they call, I will answer." **(Isaiah 65:24)** We had a new challenge, however, in that teaching work was full-time and, although a roof over our heads was provided, we had a young family with another arrival expected at any time. We had no pay for the work, but free rooms and heat were provided and we had to believe that God would send in money to feed ourselves.

We met Bill Turner at this point, in an outpouring of the Spirit at Leek in 1966. This meeting started a friendship with one of God's prophets, which has lasted. At the time, we had a real need of money. We knew Elsie's mother was coming over to be there at the delivery. Just before she arrived, an anonymous gift from Ireland met our desperate need. This proved, once again, that we could have confidence in following the vision of a living God. Our youngest child, Gareth, was born at the new Bible College.

The basic outline for foundation teaching was laid there also, as I put together all my lectures from my Oxford background and years of practical field experience. We also developed study exercises and produced model answers. The recordings of these lectures and the use of model answers, in 1992, provided us with a new 'Bible College at Home' system – similar to the Open University in England – which presented a whole new concept of learning. You get to choose your own course, do it at your own pace and pay for it by segments.

Furthermore, folk continue in their own local church and job, while they study, and no great academic standards are demanded to enter. It is essentially a practical course to enrich the whole Body of Christ, and bring the fullness of His power to every believer. This new vision and training has great potential for following-up revivals, as we later found in Ireland. After proving its worth in that country, we have now taken it on audio tape to USA, Australia and Singapore.

During this time, we still maintained links with fellowships, as well as relatives, in Northern Ireland – most of summer '66 was spent with Elsie's parents. Then, in September 1966, the Lord made it clear that our work in England was not yet finished, although we were soon to begin a new outreach to Newcastle, in Northern Ireland, where the drug problem had reached a peak in the seaside crowds.

In April 1967, the Holy Spirit gave us a nudge to make a new move. The Lord seemed to be showing us that we were to move from the college at the end of the term. The pioneer work at Wirksworth was now standing on its own feet and the initial stages of this training centre had been passed, through the provision of others. The first three students were being launched into the field at the end of the term.

The Lord made it clear that I should leave and promised a wider ministry – although the exact geographical location of our new centre was not yet fixed. Three new students had joined us this term, and already souls were being saved. We asked our friends in Ireland for prayer that we might be led to the place of God's choice for us. The Lord answered very quickly.

At Dungannon, we were privileged to renew fellowship with a pig farmer, Ernie Busby, to whom the Lord had granted an increasing ministry to the sick. One sister, who had previously had a kidney removed by the surgeon's knife, at a subsequent medical examination, claimed that it had been replaced by the power of God!

Newcastle, Co. Down, was to prove the beginning of training young people on Summer Mission work, which we had been teaching in the classrooms in England. Here we were face to face with satanic forces and violence which we had not met before. I was grateful to our praying friends for upholding us.

Thousands of pieces of literature were distributed in Newcastle at peak season. Over thirty-five children, and several adults and teenagers, found the Lord. At the weekend 'coffee-bars' we met some of the roughest types we had yet spoken to in the whole British Isles.

Of the hundreds that came in, our team retained some vivid personal impressions of great need – there was the mainline heroin addict, who threw away six pounds' worth of drugs on the spot; one who walked in, clad in tiger skin and waving a tomahawk!; Joe, from Loughgall – who was saved, baptised in the Spirit, and in the sea, and returned to his home and a decent job; Catholics from Dublin sitting next to Protestants from the Shankill Road, Belfast, and both seeking the same Saviour; those who had been sleeping rough for months without adequate food or drink, who came and found, "you were the first not to slam the door in our faces and we felt the love of Jesus." A whole family came to Christ in a day, as the Holy Spirit moved in the midst.

What a relief it was to go back to England – to do a pioneering work in Wiltshire, in the town of Trowbridge. A sister provided us with a home there for the period. Her husband was a perfect gentleman in God. Although fairly well off, when he met me with my tattered shirt, he purposely went to his cabinet and got a frayed utility article, that would match mine! Such sensitivity to the lot of the poor preacher is rare among God's people. When preachers are rich, they criticise them for being 'onto a good thing' or for being 'lazy' when they are poor. Either way, it is important to be willing to lose your reputation with Jesus. **(Philippians 2)**

When I came back to Ireland, we had a desire to have our own house, particularly as our eldest child, Michael, reached school age. With winter approaching, the caravan was too damp for the whole family. At this critical time, God stepped in. While staying with Elsie's mother, the phone rang – "You will be sorry to hear that your aunt, Margaret Boyes, has died. You may be interested to know, however, that she mentioned you in her will." I was glad I had put things right before she passed on to be with the Lord. "Excuse me, " I asked incredulously, "but did she mention a figure?"

"Just a small amount," the lawyer commented, "the legacy is only for ten thousand pounds!" I thought I was rich for life. We were living on a very small weekly sum. When the will went through probate, with the available money we were able to buy a house and take possession almost at once, although our furniture was primitive.

We regarded the supply of such needs as a direct answer to prayer. To be able to buy a house without a mortgage – just one hundred yards from the primary school – had to be the Lord's provision, in accord with His vision for our lives.

Where would we find a work place? We made contact with a local shopping centre, and I set up an office there, using the rest of the money, when it came through, to equip our outreach ministry in Ireland. From our new office and home, we laid the foundations for the later Charismatic outpouring.

When the crusades took off and we needed to look after the converts, I used the lectures we had done at Kirkby, recorded on sound tapes. Although we had seen outpourings of the Spirit, we had learned in England that this would require a trained army of labourers in the field.

Now, in Ireland, the Lord had given me a further vision of a harvest at hand. Not everyone shared that vision with me. It was a radical new departure to see Catholics blessed, as well as our traditional work among Protestants. This would require a whole new approach – and lead to a real loss of 'respectability' among our Pentecostal friends. We met an increasing hunger among young people – both Catholic and Protestant alike – for spiritual reality in Christ.

We had some response to the correspondence course, and a series of teaching meetings in the Railway Mission, in a Protestant area of Belfast. Ultimately, evangelism is a matter of God using men, not methods; and despite the new equipment we had – which made it possible for us to touch twice, or even three times, as many people every mission – I felt the need for prayer, that a deep work might be done by the Holy Ghost in individual lives.

We are "living epistles, read and known of all men." I expanded this vision, when contacting friends in June 1968, with a new concept of being 'Christians', rather than 'Protestants' or 'Catholics'. This was new to the way of thinking in Ulster.

We also introduced a new meeting format. Although we did not despise the large meetings – which were very much a pattern of Ulster evangelism – we seemed to be seeing more results, at that moment, from the less expensive, and more personal appeal of, gatherings in the house or cottage – both for 'body ministry' and individual outreach. We began to pray to raise up more of this type of meeting in Ulster. It seemed to be the pattern of New Testament evangelism, and appeared to be His leading for our outreach at that time.

Those who are coming to Christ, have shown a tremendous tendency to enter immediately into deep blessing. This was amply demonstrated in the final meeting of the Mountain Lodge mission on Easter Tuesday – where the presence of the Lord was so real that four and a half hours slipped by before we were aware of the time, and several young people entered into blessings of a nature similar to previous revival power. This outpouring of the Spirit occurred before that Church was machine-gunned by terrorists and four of its leading elders cut down in cold blood. God often visits His people to prepare them to face severe testing in the period that follows.

A new prophetic vision was given me in January 1969. I began to write to our prayer partners, "Looking back over the past year as a whole, I am happy to say that we have been enabled to outreach to new areas, both in England and in Ulster, while at the same time we have been presented with the challenge of the Catholic majority in Ireland, towards whom there is often an attitude, 'They can never be won, as they don't want the Gospel.' If we are prepared to sacrifice however – for these people are generally very poor – and have a conviction that our gospel includes miracles for body, as well as soul, we have found that there has been a real readiness on their part to believe."

I feel that something must be wrong if three quarters of the preachers with the power of God are only touching one quarter of Ireland's population. Revival doesn't come to lazy people, but to those who are in the work of God – and if you are faithful in what God has given you to do, then he takes you onwards to the next step.

Unknown to me, the greatest revival in Irish history was about to break. It was because of the vision of reaching the lost and the poor that the Lord was calling us to a key role. All our training in England and Ireland was about to be tested in a national revival of the power of God – and Civil War in Ulster.

11

New Wineskins

What in essence is the vision for this last day revival? We read in **Acts 3:19**, "Repent therefore, and turn again, that your sins may be blotted out, that times of refreshing may come from the presence of the Lord."

Early in 1971, one of my friends was given a vision of two groups of people shouting at each other in Ulster. One was coloured black and the other coloured white. These colours represented Catholic and Protestant traditions. Suddenly rain came down from heaven, and all those coloured white, became black, as the water washed away the whitewash over their bodies. The Holy Spirit was demanding a radical change of heart and not outward adherence to God – and showing that both sides needed this change, rather than just the one.

For a long time, however, people in Ireland considered that it was merely to be a renewal of old traditions, rather than a radical change that the Holy Spirit was bringing.

What is the difference between 'renewal' and 'revival'? Renewal is a situation in which there is a certain amount of life beginning afresh in a dead church. The teaching is that people stay within their old church. They work for the renewal of the church. Now, revival often begins in a church that has had life, but is 'dead'. This can be compared to Israel and the picture of a valley of dry bones, (**Ezekiel 37:2**) – there are "very many, very dry."

The context of revival is not merely the renewal of the old human system, but a return to the New Testament and God's original pattern for His people. That may mean a totally new organisation, it may mean a totally new concept. Also, it is sovereignly of God. It is directed to blessing the Kingdom of God. It is not primarily to shore up a human organisation. Many people in the 'Charismatic Renewal' were trying to use the Holy Ghost to shore up the system of established churches. God's idea was to return the church to the New Testament pattern.

As we saw it in the 1970s, what God was trying to say was, "New wine must go into new wineskins." (**Mark 2:22 NIV**) 'New wineskins' does not necessarily mean a new system. It means a stretching, a wineskin that can stretch. In other words, if the old system can stretch, it can absorb the move of the Spirit. If it cannot stretch – and most people don't, because they settle into bondage/routine/habit – then you have a problem of conflict.

In the 1970s, God led me to read, in **Acts 19:9**, that Paul, "separated the disciples." He showed me that the Holy Spirit did not cause a division. There was an already existing split, which the Holy Spirit brought to the surface. There were already those who were content with being Jews. There were others who wanted more of God. Just so, here in Ireland, there were those who were content with the status quo, and there were those who wanted more. In that situation, you try to live in peace together as much as you can.

The move of the Holy Ghost brought about a problem, later. Those who were content, felt threatened by those who wanted more. If that is the position, it can be better that they separate, because otherwise the two remaining together would fight all the time. Finney, in his book on revival, suggested that it is better if the two split, because the two can agree individually. (**Matthew 18:19**) God will hear prayer of those agreeing, whereas He cannot hear the disagreement of the two staying together.

One man expressed it to me in Newry at the time, "I've been in 'The Way' eleven years and never felt the need of a fresh experience of the Spirit." I remember replying, "That is the trouble, brother. You <u>have</u> been stuck in the way!"

My own position is that I think no system is going to be the final one – short of the return of the Lord Jesus. There has to be a humble approach to these things, and a readiness for fresh revelation. The ideal is for each individual to live in personal, continuous renewal, so that when the next move of God comes, they're free to move into it.

Revival has been first in the lives of Christians, then in the lives of others. I, personally, decided to seek the Lord at an early age, and began to read the bible. From the bible I came to see certain truths, which were helpful when I was at Oxford, where I was able to compare these with the history of the Church.

At Theological College, God began to talk about the cost of revival – it meant the end of my career as an Established Church minister – and the end of the financial security and social position which went with it. Having paid a price for being baptised in water, I was prepared to move on to the baptism in the Spirit and speaking in tongues. Then, as I began to seek God in fasting and praying, people praying with me began to confirm that God had chosen me as one of His instruments.

When God again began to speak to me about moving into the area of teaching, and in schools, God revealed the fact that He was bringing fresh truth to a new generation and that revival takes a team of people. In England, young people from broken homes found the love of the Lord – their science teacher then looked after them.

In the school in rural Ireland, I had a burden, because there was such a lack of knowledge of things of the Spirit. When we prayed and fasted and taught with the other teachers, there came a deep conviction of sin through the Word, so that the seed was sown deeply, for six months, before revival ever came.

The morning that the Lord spoke to me from Jonah, I stopped praying and started moving – sending away for booklets for the people that I thought would be saved. But even then, I wasn't expecting such a huge move. When the converts came in, they immediately led one another into the revival. As the revival grew, other people took it on.

It seems this has been a pioneering ministry – of breaking through for others to be blessed. In coming to Chard, we were among the first people to learn, through fasting and prayer, the biblical concept of the ministry of the whole Body. Then we had an outpouring of gifts of the Spirit with the Irish evangelist. From that, we also saw missionary movement, and my own calling to my life's work in Ireland.

Continuous renewal also means personal contact with God. When a believer begins to fall away, he or she tends to go for what God did last year, or the year before, when they were in contact with Him. People build up on their past experience a sense of security – but the only security you have is Jesus, who is Life. Eternal life is a person and continuous contact with that person – abiding in Him. It's not the business of having had an experience in times past. God is always moving on – and He's a Creator, so do not be surprised if new things come up all the time.

Generally, when each new revival comes, it takes some good parts from the old, but then, when the old fight it, the two go their separate ways and they both lose out because of bitterness. The old often has truth and experience which the new needs. With the Charismatic move, the Pentecostals were the old move, refusing to help.

At this time in Ireland, a vision was given of a plant tied to an old, dead stake, but as the plant grew, the stake was restricting it, instead of helping it. That was a potent lesson that the new revival needs the old stake, but it must not be tied to the old. Often, when this persecution starts, the new people don't have any time for the old people and just chuck them out – that is wrong. It is equally wrong to bottle up the new experiences and limit God with the old format.

The New Testament equivalent were the Judaizers. The main move was with the Jews in Jerusalem, then

God moved to Antioch, and there you had the new concept of being called 'Christian', (**Acts 11:26**) – not just a new sect or renewal of Judaism, but a whole new concept – and out of that, Paul's ministry was birthed.

Into that situation went Barnabas, a very gracious man – he does not 'fight rings round him' and he encourages the new converts. He welcomes Paul, who has been a persecutor. (**Acts 9:26-27**) 'Grace' is a very apt word to describe Barnabas' actions. He protects Mark, when he lets the Lord down. (**Acts 15:37-39**) He is the key to renewal, although Paul is the more obvious leader of revival and of the formation of the Christian church.

Barnabas remains an apostle, but loses leadership in this new concept. At first, it is 'Barnabas and Paul'. (**Acts 11:26**) Later the order becomes, 'Paul and Barnabas', (**Acts 13:41-46**), as Paul goes ahead with the whole new revelation. Barnabas was content to let this happen. We need those with a gracious, Barnabas ministry today in renewal – as well as those with Paul's more radical revival and forming of new churches.

God was about to show me into this new church experience through a change in my circumstances – from travelling, to sitting still in one place and working out a new church form in the house, based on New Testament teaching. (**Acts 8:3**) This began with a dramatic new development. Renewal is the beginning of new life, but that life must mature.

Each new thrust forward must be followed by consolidation. That point is critical in the history of revival, yet is hardly touched by those who merely emphasise the forward thrusts. The travelling evangelist must also catch the vision of the resident pastor, if he wishes to move onward to apostolic calling and the fathering of other churches. Such was the essence of our next vision.

12

Consolidation at Holywood

"We had an outpouring of the Spirit with five thousand decisions in just a few months," one American pastor told me. "We did not consolidate the move and we now have six people left in the Church from that revival move in miracles and power."

Sheer exhaustion, and blindness to the different roles of pastor and evangelist, lead to the breakdown of many revivals. Today we need apostles to combine these two roles, and plant churches to win nations.

My own call to this ministry came publicly in a tent meeting in Millisle, Northern Ireland. Obviously, with several churches started in England and Ireland, this was the confirmation of my own experience in God and of a definite policy of spiritual warfare.

One of the great dangers of victory in warfare – both

natural and spiritual – is the over-stretching that leads to a breakdown of momentum. The inevitable counter-attack can be quite devastating. This proved a very real factor in the North African campaign, between the Germans and the English, under Montgomery – until the battle of El Alamein was fought, under properly prepared conditions and planning. The fact that the British army was invigorated and organised well before the attack was launched, proved decisive in the war. El Alamein became a sustained victory.

From the moment I was given foreknowledge of bloodshed to come in Ulster, I had been waging a campaign at a national level, in accordance with the vision given. Our small home and office at Glengormley had been the centre of outreach operations for the Ulster crusades, but now the new move of God needed planning and leaders, and this meant training.

The number of decisions made for Christ, alone demanded a major follow-up operation, and for the next four years I sent a personal letter to every adult, and five letters to every child who made a commitment in our outreaches. In addition I sent details to every minister in the areas where they lived. Thank God for the clergy who followed up these contacts, but I must, in honesty, say that most never bothered to reply.

We saw some thirty per cent increase in the number of adults enquiring between 1967 and 1970, with some five hundred children making decisions in 1968 and 1969 – when sixty adults were also baptised in water. An equal number were baptised in the Holy Spirit each year.

The number of decisions was multiplied during the Beach Mission work at Newcastle, where thirty five found

Christ in an open-air meeting one night – when a man threw away his stick and walked, in the healing power of Christ.

Another night, a young boy was struck down by God's power and was unable to move – until he had returned the pencils he stole at our coffee bar! We believe that God moved in judgement, so that the Church would walk in the fear of the Lord – as well as the comfort of the Holy Ghost. This holiness side of God, seen in judgement, caused the Roman Centurion to believe, in Paul's first missionary journey. (**Acts 16**) Is the Church ready for it now?

In 1971, for instance, we had about a thousand people praying for the ministry and a breakthrough occurred in our seaside work. The Lord brought together a whole, unexpected, new team for Newcastle, and over one hundred and thirty professions of salvation were made, by young and old. I was laid up, just beforehand, with exhaustion through the work, so this was a double answer to prayer.

The time had obviously come, however, to match this work with an adequate team. The Lord made it possible for us to rent for a year a Fellowship Centre at Demesne Road, Holywood. We opened it on September 19th, as a community from which we could work, training those with a definite call to evangelism. This new Bible Training Centre in Holywood enabled me – with brothers David Matthews and Marcel Desmet – to raise up an Apostolic Team for the needs of the whole land.

I began to see this new vision as early as 1962. At that time, throughout the country, there was a thrilling move of the Holy Ghost – which was not only leading hundreds to miracles of salvation and healing, but bringing believers back to the bible and church ministry of the Body.

This created a demand for Holy Ghost teaching ministry far beyond the capacity of one man, or even two. Other young men, who had been baptised in the Spirit, were asking the question, "Why can we not train for full gospel ministry in Ireland?" The Lord brought together the fellowship at Demesne Road to meet these needs – within a family atmosphere. The house acted as a home meeting for local people, enjoying a Holy Ghost ministry, irrespective of denominational ties – similar to the many others raised up all over the country.

At the same time, through its resident evangelistic team, it provided a centre for the training of young people all over the province, who had proved their calling in local meetings, and now wished to gain further experience of mobile work – as the young Timothy did with the older Paul. In addition, the valuable results gained from correspondence courses were supplemented at the house, by weekend and other special teaching sessions.

Quietly and consistently, the work went forward in Holywood, where we had regular contact with army children – and one paratroop officer – in the local barracks. We thank God for being part of the vision of cottage meetings – where Catholics and Protestants met regularly, and saw the Spirit moving in power.

As before, this vision was born in prayer. A praying lady was used to guide us to take over that missionary training college in Holywood, on a short lease – just opposite the local primary school. God particularly blessed us with this school in Holywood – enabling the children to grow up as part of our extended family. Later, at Grammar School age, they qualified for Sullivan Upper School in Holywood – run by a Christian headmaster, with many of his staff being evangelical.

Once the lease ran out on the Bible School, we looked at a new house at 152 High Street. The building had seven bedrooms and some large reception rooms. The Pentecostal pastor who showed us round was enthusiastic and we had a little money from the sale of our Glengormley home.

"Just get the money from the bank," he advised, "I will lend you one thousand pounds meanwhile." We felt rather foolish asking the local bank for a loan, without a steady income, but God went before us. "Who is your pastor friend?" asked the bank manager, looking a little 'pale and overdrawn' at our request for a mortgage. When he heard the name of the pastor, his attitude changed.

"His brother is the current Lord Mayor of Belfast, and his business has been in property for years. How much do you want to borrow?" Fortified by this step, our prophet friend, Bill Turner, then had a vision of the exact sum needed for the house, together with traffic lights at green for 'Go'.

In June 1972, we moved into 152 High Street. This became the centre of our work in Holywood for the next fifteen years – with up to two hundred people, weekly, making their way through the home, to the large upper room at the top of the building. It certainly was sent from God.

The new facility gave us the premises for audio and video taping – which produced an electronic Bible School resource, to back the revival move with solid bible teaching. We pioneered the use of video, as we foresaw it would play an increasing part in teaching believers.

The teaching centre naturally developed into a church-planting centre. I had to modify some of my teaching notes in the light of my experiences as a pastor. Over this period we also were able to prepare studies on the whole bible, and had put some of the notes onto disks for computerised use. With the bible on computer, personal study has achieved a new dimension. We are blessed by no longer having to carry around heavy books.

Audio Visual Ministries was formed as a fully mobile bible study – like a bible college at home – where people stay in their church, do not lose their local connections and can choose what they want to learn. Our aim from the beginning was not to achieve academic standing, but to provide some more practical experience – similar to the Open University – where people are able to stay in their local environment, but receive the benefits of specialised teaching.

Using lectures from our previous training school in England, we were able to produce, in this facility, new video and audio tape talks, recorded live in Spirit-charged meetings, which we matched with duplicated notes. This enabled students to take sections of their own choice – and very cheaply.

At the end of each forty-five minute talk, we added some bible questions for personal study, and, over the years, have supplemented these with model answers. With the advent of domestic video recorders, God had given us a key to a whole new bible teaching process which would enable local church members at home to be given a sound Biblical foundation.

We believe in explaining what God was doing super-naturally from a practical and scholarly view of Scripture. This is of direct benefit to those with a desire towards church work and needing a practical way to set about it, with a balanced biblical philosophy for inquirers. The apostolic potential of this system is obvious for international mobile work, to which we have been called – but there is also a prophetic edge to the process.

We saw a powerful use of video with Tony and Marge Abram – who visited our fellowship in February, 1983. They prophesied on video that certain people watching would be healed, and we later received confirmation of this. This has already begun to happen internationally.

Like any solid structure, however, this has taken time to develop. Initially, in our time at 152 High Street, there were times of discouragement, when numbers attending were very low – often in single figures. Then, as the work grew, there were pressures of overwork and stress. For some years, we thought the answer lay in a move to larger premises.

Already, by the end of 1979, we had started believing God for new and larger premises – as the meetings filled to overflowing. As the pressures increased, however, we took seriously God's Sabbath rest of one day in the week, and we also tried to get a break on Wednesdays on a regular basis.

We were also very stretched in other meetings, as we were travelling some 500 miles every fortnight – to house meetings throughout the north of Ireland. Soon we were travelling across the Atlantic and suffering from jet lag also. A crisis came at the end of 1980. After three weeks in bed from total exhaustion through overwork, financed by the family, we went off for three weeks to Canada for a vital rest – with only seventeen meetings!

By 1984, the pressure was further accentuated by the murder of the Mountain Lodge church elders – to which we have already referred – and the very real physical threat to Pentecostal churches beginning to grip Ulster.

We were encouraged by the Darkley funerals. It was a witness to Ireland of God's power, on the media, as they forgave the murderers. I have had the privilege of standing beside the open graves of some former brothers in Christ, from Mountain Lodge, Keady, and being able to see their widows in total victory and total forgiveness of their murderers.

At the same time, the Lord was bringing international ministries to our new home, with a vision of global horizons. We were privileged to entertain men of God in our home, like David du Plessis and Sandy Thompson, with a prophetic and world-experienced insight into bible truth, which rubbed off on the family around the meal table.

Brother Bill Turner often came over from England, and the children enjoyed his fellowship. It became obvious when he said, "We have company," that a large angel had just walked into the room! Bill also had the God-given ministry of placing Holy Ghost protection on people at a distance.

Before the meeting one night, he and the children were watching a Wimbledon tennis match, where an ungodly player was beating a Christian. Bill discerned that a spiritual battle was also in progress, and proceeded to pray divine protection for the Christian – to enable him to play the game fairly. Before our very eyes, on national television, we saw a miraculous change – as the balls crawled back over the net and a dramatic reversal took place in the fortunes of the game. The children were truly sorry to see Bill go away to prepare the sermon that night – Wimbledon in the Holy Ghost was far more exciting!

Although based in Holywood, we still travelled to take meetings throughout Northern Ireland – in Enniskillen, Bangor, Castlederg, Newry, Glengormley, Larne, Craigavon, Greenisland: and also in the south of Ireland – Sligo, Carrick-on-Shannon, Ballaghadereen, Dublin: and God was with us in our travels. But this new apostolic role had its dangers also.

On the night of December 2nd, 1975, for instance, we were nearly killed after a meeting at Ballaghadereen – where one hundred Catholic people had found new assurance of salvation and a prayer language. A sister was given a warning that Satan intended to kill us that same evening.

On the way home to our family, our car skidded on black ice and plunged to the bottom of a field, six feet below the road bend. Although the car turned two somersaults and came to rest on its side, Elsie and I, by a miracle, were able to walk away unscathed. People tend to forget there is a price to pay for travelling in extended ministry, and we did thank God for His provision for our young family over this period. Those who "keep the stuff at home," are just as important as those on the front-line. **(1 Samuel 30:24)**

In 1979, around Easter, Elsie's mother passed on to be with the Lord. The family was extended by the presence of her father – a Baptist and a real Christian gentleman. Mr. Ritchie showed us how it is possible to have doctrinal differences, and still remain a community in the Lord, where service is the key attitude.

Another group of young people living in a Christian community in Belfast, came to us for regular fellowship. Later, under Graeme Hall, they set up a community in Glassdrumman, with the motto 'Simple Excellence' – where witnessing was done on a service basis.

This developed into a wonderful Christian hotel complex, near our present home, "where the mountains of Mourne sweep down to the sea." They have truly made up to us for our 'feeding' them at Holywood, by 'keeping the stuff' during our current global outreaches. We have found, in fact, that every major ministry needs a home team to back it and refresh the apostolic team when returning from the field.

However, it was with reluctance that we started a new Spirit-filled church in Holywood, and only after the failure of an attempt to plant one by another Pentecostal group. Why? Aware of my responsibility to pastor many of those who were coming to our home in Holywood for teaching, and going to no other church, we took the momentous decision to give teaching, on the basis of long-term commitment for the formation of character, and not just ministry.

It was also at this time that I had a definite vision from a leadership gathering at the Ichthus Fellowship in London, that it was vital we rested a while from the frantic front-line campaign activity, if we were to resume a forward move again in power.

There comes a physical moment for recuperation after a national revival – as with Elijah in **1 Kings:18,19** – when a leader needs to quieten down to hear the still, small voice of the Holy Spirit's leading. The Lord Himself knew this and, in **Mark 1:35**, set aside time in a moment of success, to see the divine program afresh.

What did we learn from this settled time? While a certain financial security is achieved by regular commitment, pastoring has its own problems – especially of living with your own mistakes!

Very quickly it became obvious that a whole new discipline of dealing with problems had to be taken on board – because if they were not quickly settled, parties were formed round the aggrieved person, and, instead of just one or two, you had to deal with many people. The pastor, I learned, does best not to let problems grow, to the point where the flock suffers from one person's lack of willingness to change his or her behaviour.

What was the philosophy of this new move of the Spirit? Our aim at Holywood was to produce a whole prophetic church, directly in touch with God by revelation ministry, with a solid grasp of the written word. This general ministry was gradually achieved by the input from apostles, prophets and evangelists – working as a team, to make the body mature enough to minister to itself and others. **(Ephesians 4:11-13)**

The emphasis – in times when in leadership we faced the very real danger of losing our lives – was to produce a group with dependence directly on God. By teaching and practising prayer, based on expecting immediate revelation from God, each person began to believe for the fullness of the Gifts, **(Ephesians 3:17-20)**, for the benefit of others. The Spirit is given by God, without measure, **(John 3:34)** – the **KJV** "unto him" is not in the Greek. In Holywood, this had two important effects.

139

Firstly, a church was formed in which the supernatural became normal. One new convert was afraid to be baptised because of an old fear of water. Aware that others regularly talked to the Lord, she asked Jesus to personally visit her about this problem. She was not surprised when, next day, He walked into her home and reassured her. While she came out rejoicing, we slipped and nearly lost her husband, who was also being baptised!

Secondly, this atmosphere, of spiritual children growing up into maturity, led to the emergence of two other groups at Larne and Portadown, some thirty miles east and west of Holywood. While this may have deprived Holywood of some good leaders, it certainly benefited the kingdom of God.

The danger of many house churches lies in their very success as a caring 'family of God' – without a vision for expansion. Unity was underlined by Easter and autumn national gatherings for the next few years at Castlewellan Castle. This residential weekend proved marvellous in giving the wives a rest from some chores and the whole body the benefit of specialist ministry.

The Ichthus Fellowship in London also soon proved a source of rich ministry, cemented in the period of intensive prayer for the healing of Roger Forster's son Chris, from leukaemia in the lymph glands. This miracle has stood the test of time and triggered an association of Holywood with this supernatural and bible-based work in London.

Did we neglect our local witness? Far from it. We began to engage in spiritual warfare for the town of Holywood. Being the only 'full gospel' group in Holywood at this time, meant that we were challenged to pray for a change in the spiritual atmosphere of the area. Quite literally, over a period of years, the local ministry was radically changed towards Charismatic gifts.

We developed the new concept then of a city revival – where the churches would work together. As a result, Rev. Trevor Dearing graciously accepted an invitation to take a weekend series in a large local hall, and the mainline denominational ministers were thrilled to have those converted fed back to them to swell their flocks. A local Presbyterian told me that this was the first crusade where he had been told of a convert within a few hours of that decision being made.

We also moved as a team with ministers throughout the country. For instance, we made sure, when people joined Holywood, that we found out just how they stood in relation to their former fellowships. One man, who had a debt outstanding, was asked to square it up. Shortly afterwards, his wife was admitted to hospital with a fatal condition – and he was glad to have a church who prayed and fasted, seeing a fatal disease healed right there in the hospital intensive care unit.

Our time at Holywood also proved a training ground for scriptural ministries. We promoted the teaching of meeting as 'Christians' – not merely Catholics or Protestants – with a bible foundation in home groups. This led, in nearby Bangor, to a distinctive 'Discipleship Movement,' which broadened and changed to a major move in the east end of Belfast, of the larger Christian Fellowship Church. After prayer, this church developed a less controlling leadership philosophy and befriended the John Wimber early crusades in the City of Belfast.

We had wonderful fellowship with the leaders of this

group who moved into Holywood. We have been delighted to see their subsequent progress in church planting in the north of Ireland. We see ourselves as merely part of the Kingdom of God, which allows several groups to work harmoniously in the same town.

We did not give up on our holiday seaside outreaches. Holywood was also the birthplace of training and outreach groups to Millisle – where half of east Belfast traditionally takes its summer holiday – after the Newcastle work ended.

At Millisle, the local Elim Church, under pastor Walker Gorman, gave us encouragement. With the late Sandy Thompson, who lived with us for some time, much of the earlier blessing at Newcastle was duplicated in this new venue, with even greater supernatural happenings.

How did this new vision work out? I believe that an apostle needs local training, and that God rewards faithfulness with a larger calling. That has been the way this vision has worked in our lives. God makes changes in the 'fullness of time'.

13

Called to World Outreach

One of Ireland's main exports is people. Anything that happens in Ireland is going to have world repercussions, because of the influence of emigration abroad. Yet, when I heard the command to make Christian disciples throughout the world, **(Matthew 28:19)**, there was a right time to obey this vision also.

Revival was never meant to be inward looking, from the time when Jesus said, **(Acts 1:8)** "But you will receive power when the Holy Spirit comes on you; and you will be my witnesses in Jerusalem, and in all Judea and Samaria, and to the ends of the earth."

We are to be His witnesses at home and then unto the end of the world. The concern which we felt for the poor in Ireland, had led us to pray that God would keep His promise to give us the "heathen for our inheritance." **(Psalm 2:8)** This promise He had kept. Now He added "the uttermost parts of the earth for our possession."

How did this happen? In the same unhurried way our miracles occur.

The move to world evangelism really began with the outreach to America. A Presbyterian Minister and his wife came to Ireland and were baptised in water and the Holy Spirit. Their church, in Yakima, Washington State, paid for us to come to America in November 1977. In turn they asked that we preach and repay them from the offerings. Over fifty decisions for Christ were made during the four weeks of meetings, and others were baptised in the Holy Spirit.

Thereafter, we made many friends in Yakima and have visited there periodically over fifteen years. There has been a blessing every time we have gone. By 1994, we were able to establish AVM (USA) there, as a non-profit corporation, to supply books and teaching tapes for all of the USA, including Hawaii.

In 1984, I had a vision of the whole dry valley being filled with water and God pouring out his Spirit. Then we were taken into a Pentecostal Church – the Word of Life. The pastor of that church had a vision for a city-wide revival.

Again this idea of teamwork was emphasised, where no individual is seen, but the Lord is revealed through people working together in a pastoral role. Harold Eberle and the Winepress Ministry from that church, have also blessed us with their books and teaching in Ireland.

Local unity makes possible a city-wide outreach. The local Yakima churches had a crusade with Mario Murillo in 1991. Twenty churches were prepared to take part, and booked the large Sundome Stadium. All the pastors got together and made us welcome on a packed platform.

They worked so well together that they had crowds of several thousand people in the meeting place, with four hundred responding to the call for prayer over three nights. The first night covered all the expenses because of the pooling of resources. This, by American standards, was brilliant and unexpected. I was privileged to be at the meeting and to begin to see that vision of the valley flowing being fulfilled.

Then, in October 1991, again God met the thousands of dollars needed to minister in USA, Australia and Singapore – with money left to us in the will of a deceased farmer friend. Again, there has been a timing on purchasing our new home in Northern Ireland, and the challenge to turn our backs on this new security, to bless the needy people round the globe. We are seeking to serve and up-build the local churches. This must be the motive for real ministry to the Body of Christ.

One lady, at a 'Women's Aglow' meeting in Yakima, asked for a vision for her future ministry. The Lord showed her washing dishes with her husband. Although this was hardly the word she expected, she showed her gratitude to us the following year, by publicly hugging us. She had spent this time at home, at the sink, when suddenly her husband passed on to be with the Lord.

It is important to do good while there is time, and to discern the perfect will of God. The key is to have a servant heart. It is also important to rise above your circumstances and think of others. God can work all things for good, **(Romans 8:28),** provided you get better and not bitter.

Within the Holywood church, for instance, there was a

lady whose husband on several occasions, released her to travel – to Israel, Russia and even Red China. Despite alcoholic problems in the family, and great poverty, she became a missionary, with her Spirit-filled singing, and testimony to the difference that the Lord Jesus can make in any circumstances. She held prisoners in Siberia spellbound, as she described what the Lord had done in her home. Let the Holy Spirit open the doors.

How does He do it ?

Australia opened up to us through a person who was baptised in the Spirit many years ago, when we were in Ardoyne, Belfast. He lived near Perth, and invited us out to speak, and we included Australia in our world travel.

Then we came into contact with folk who invited us to Newcastle, near the eastern side of Australia, and many doors opened up to us in western Australia, around Perth. We saw the same vision for revival among the people in that area.

God seems to work through key people. Some of our Australian friends were supporting the work of Eric Huber in Singapore – Singapore opened up to us. There is obviously a continuous revival going on there – with a real emphasis on teaching and scholarship – in the Anglican Church, backed by local house groups.

Is it all hard work? Do we also have some holiday locations? Hawaii opened up more as a result of the friendship, which a minister visiting Ireland had, with one of the pastors. We found that we could fly there at very little extra expense on top of going to Seattle, and so there is a holiday side to that too.

What about travel sickness and jet lag? Can God do something here? About four or five years ago, in Yakima, a lady in the Word of Life Church said to us, that the Lord had told her to tell us that we were not going to have any more jet lag. Previously, we would suffer jet lag for four weeks after a flight across the Atlantic, but now there is no problem. It seems funny – now we can arrive at places before the time we left, just go to bed at the local bedtime, and get up in the morning as normal.

How has the world ministry developed? Obviously, the time involved in travelling brought pressure on our local church situation in Holywood, despite the miracle provision of God and His obvious calling. Inevitably, there came a crisis in the amount of time needed to be spent abroad, as against the pastoral concerns in Northern Ireland.

I should say that the vision gradually grew. I felt the call to Ireland, but to a degree I had limited that call. I had a call to Apostleship but did not realise that it was to the whole world. I was in for a rude shock. Bill Turner, our prophet friend, saw the Devil, himself, come against me! At first I couldn't understand that – but of course he is the Prince of the World and we had been fighting other demons, as preparation. You fight your way through in the supernatural. (**Matt 12:29**)

When we were in the Potteries in England, with Pastor Wilson in 1992, he told me that victory had been won in the heavenlies for Elsie and me. There had been a fight through and victory won in the heavenlies, because people had been praying, and the Devil had been overcome to that degree – in the heavenlies first. God then confirmed this call by a strange meeting, as a result of seeing my Holywood Bank Manager. He sent me on my way with the final word, "You must meet my bishop friend from

Seattle."

When we met the bishop, in Yakima, he stated that God is putting together a man-child to rule the world, **(Revelations 12:15)** – Christians will be called upon in a ruling situation. For this calling, the bishop prophesied that I would have to die not only to my sin, but also to my abilities. This would be a very painful death. He went on to tell me that I had received this calling in the Millisle tent, on the very month it was given to me by Sandy Thompson – although he had not been there!

Rather than moving merely on prophecy, however, Elsie and I waited on the Lord for a word from Himself, in our daily time with Him. **(Romans 10:17)** This came while we were on a caravan holiday near Kilkeel, with the same force as we had experienced in our original call to Scotland, from **Micah 4:10**. This time He spoke to us from the **Micah 2:10 (AV)**, "Arise ye, and depart; for this is not your rest."

This was followed by friends suggesting that we needed to act on this precise direction, and pledging the backing of the Christian Community at Glassdrumman Hotel for our decision. It was a step of faith to forego our regular salary. We had already proved that where God guides, He will also provide. We had to think in practical terms about timing – there's a timing for revival which is sovereign – and that would mean that our family would be settled into new homes.

The marriage of our three children to three Spirit-filled partners, and the passing of Elsie's father to be with the Lord, relieved us of much domestic responsibility. The church at Holywood, however, was centred in our large house. Removal of the church to a local hall, was followed by the miracle of the sale of our house for cash, at a time of stagnant house economy in Ireland. It went for ten times the price we had paid originally, and enabled us to update our car and caravan.

After renting a house for a year – while we went abroad – God did a second miracle in finding us a new home at Annalong – just next to the Christian community who had pledged to support us. This lovely home, "where the mountains of Mourne sweep down to the sea," had every facility for which we had prayed. Although it was time to put aside my involvement with Holywood, as an apostle it was vital for me to have had pastoral experience there.

Apostles and evangelists can come into a church situation with immediate 'solutions', or lack of follow-up, but, in the **Ephesians 4** summary, the apostle's work is as part of a team, with the pastors, for the general up-building. Unless you have actually pastored, this is difficult. In the past, because I was involved in pioneering work, there was nothing already set up and I did not have to co-operate with many people.

How would we be able to spend another year abroad, without a regular salary? The Lord touched the heart of an American pastor to sponsor a prolonged visit to the United States; and another one in Australia, to cover our entry there – and then a lawyer phoned me to say that one of our faithful prayer people had left us enough money in his estate to make a year's visit possible. The timing was marvellous, as we had already decided to obey God's call.

Waiting on God for one year at a time, has been the way in which He seems to have led – but we are full of expectation that He wants to bless others with revival. And the best is yet to be.

In fact, in Hawaii, in 1991, Paul Cain called us out in a large meeting – "God is going to do a new thing, with whole nations to be saved. The couple from Ireland, here, are to continue to be based in that land, where they are to be part of an even larger thing that God is going to do." That clear direction led us to the purchase of the Annalong home, and has led to a larger vision of a mighty move of the Spirit yet to come.

The Lord seems to be leading "from glory to glory." What have we learned from seeing this vision of God moving ?

14

Continuing Vision

We have identified some stages to this move as seen in **Ezekiel 37**.

I summarise them here, to underline what we have learned in our walk with God:

1 **Dryness** among the people of God. This was a feature of what we saw in schools where I taught, in Scotland, in the early days of our marriage, and of large country districts of Ireland in the 1960s – **v.2**, "bones that were very dry."

2 **A vision from God**, coming with prophetic power – **v.1**, "The hand of the Lord was upon me, and he brought me out by the Spirit of the Lord." In our marriage, we saw that God alone proved the basis of our later security in our relationship, calling, and supply of every need. Because this Word is so important a key, there must be absolute surrender to it. Our last call to travel, for instance, did away with

all security from regular income, and, at our advanced age, took faith to receive.

3 **Prophecy and telling out what God has said – v.4**, "Then he said to me, 'Prophesy to these bones, "Hear the word of the Lord."'" This is not only the key to salvation, (**Romans 10:10**), baptism in the Spirit, (**Acts 10:46**), and healing; but has become a word to rally support and heal the divisions in the Body of Christ, caused by hurts of the past. Jesus correctly said, "My sheep hear my voice, and they follow me." (**John 10**) The Body, coming together as Christians, has brought unity to Ireland and seems to be the key to world-wide revival.

4 **Power of the wind of the Spirit giving life to this unified body – v.5**, "I will make breath enter you, and you will come to life." We have seen this supernatural work of God in the Charismatic outpouring of the 1970s. The emphasis of the move must remain on the glory of God. Revival is not meant to be prostituted to serve a denomination, or publicity for one individual ministry – eg. the vision of the cat, referred to in Chapter 1. The new move of God will be among those with a pure desire to see His glory.

5 **An army was formed** from the resurrected skeletons – **v.10**, "They came to life and stood up on their feet – a vast army." God is bringing revival, to do battle against the demonic world forces opposed to His Kingdom on earth. Revival is setting the scene for a dramatic increase in the supernatural. On one side is the increasing power of God, and on the other, gathering darkness and supernatural challenge from demons.

In the story of the ten virgins, (**Matthew 25**), all ten had oil, but only five had enough to enter the marriage feast, when the Bridegroom came at midnight. In the time of trouble that lies ahead, the Church must experience this revival in order to be equipped for survival. God grant His people be willing in that day. (**Psalm 110:3**)

For myself and my house, we have found it best to serve the Lord. Humbly, this has been a simple testimony, like Paul, (**Acts 26:19**), "I was not disobedient to the heavenly vision."

If God has given you a heavenly vision, if God has given you a calling, and He has called you to pray – do not be disobedient. Obey what God has given you and, down the line, you're going to prove that His way is the best way. We have found this after half a century. To Him be all the glory.

Prayer

Father, I thank you that Your calling is to go forward into obedience, into communion, and into victory. Lord, we may start in a small way, but You have called us into increasing ministry of power, and of Your love, and of all the good things You want to do in Jesus.

We pray, Lord Jesus, that if anyone has received a call, has not yet been saved, has not yet gone into that ministry calling that they have received from You, that they may do so, and might move by Your mighty power. Lord, we thank You for all that You are doing, and we ask, right now, that You will move in a supernatural way to glorify Your name. Amen.

Matthew 28:19-20 – "Therefore go and make disciples of all nations, baptising them in the name of the Father and of the Son and the Holy Spirit, and teaching them to obey everything I have commanded you. And surely I am with you always, to the very of the age."

Definition of Audio Visual Ministries (AVM)

Audio Visual Ministries in the United Kingdom is a charity offering a unique system of bible teaching. It brings expert practical instruction through the use of modern media, to every Christian who wants deeper study, but cannot afford the time or money to go to a residential college. It is based in the Newcastle area of Northern Ireland, and works through a ministry, built up over 35 years in Ireland, America, Australia and the Far East.

Over thirty teaching courses on audio tapes are currently available to help individual students – with a selection of video backup on such subjects as Prophecy, Divine Healing, Counselling and Church Growth, made at special weekend conference sessions in Ireland.

It also includes computer software, giving access to different bible versions and study books, under licence from 'Biblesoft' of America; and teaching booklets on 'Life in the Spirit', 'Divine Healing' and 'Spirit Warfare' produced from tapes made on these subjects and used in Europe, USA and the Far East.

There is a current radio outreach from United Christian Broadcasters in Stoke on Trent and Vision 864 in Ireland, with over a million potential Irish listeners.

Design of Audio Visual Ministries

AVM operates under the prayerful direction of Keith Gerner. Keith has a vision for every believer coming into the fullness of Christ under apostolic ministry. (**Ephesians 4:11-13**)

AVM is recognised as a UK Charity – No X 8828. This enables it to serve the whole Body of Christ, with trustees and audited accounts. AVM has also set up indigenous teaching facilities in Asia, America and Australia, also under local auspices as recognised charities. This enables it to have a world wide vision, with the minimum of office costs to each branch, and local accountability.

AVM (UK) is currently achieving its aims by:

• Radio outreach and visitation throughout Ireland

• Teaching seminars, which are promoting local ministries, and offering a resource centre of 3,000 tapes, in Belfast, for those wishing to further their calling in God – the product of over 20 years practical experience here.

• Local church teaching sessions, backed by inexpensive booklets and tapes.

• An opportunity for local ministries to go abroad, backed by AVM in USA, Australia and Singapore, and to receive sound ministry from abroad. This imported ministry has already been proven locally by AVM in these countries.

Direction of Audio Visual Ministries

In order to further these aims, AVM is now seeking:-

• **Circle of Prayer Partners**

AVM can only go forward through regular and informed intercession, and so intend to publish a prayer letter for those who are prepared to bring this work before the Lord, and to make a donation to cover administration of this ministry.

• **Committed supporters**

These are grateful for what has been achieved in the past. They wish to free ministry from financial burdens by giving, in order to enable the last commission of Christ – to teach and make disciples – to be worked out in the period before His return.

In view of taxpayers being able to reclaim UK revenue payments, and the current peace initiative in Ireland, the time is now for a commitment to this process, by individuals in the UK with a vision for world revival. We are actually doing the job already on the ground world-wide, but we cannot continue it without teamwork.

• **Christians wishing to expand the vision of AVM**

Those who may wish to see this ministry expand, by enrolling the necessary staff to enable leadership to concentrate on the Word of God and prayer, rather than spending time on raising funds. (**Acts 6**) Those who have already proved the worth of this ministry – and really do believe that Christ is soon returning, and that there is a harvest to be reaped – may enter a partnership in this harvest, which will lead to eternal blessing and satisfaction.

Catch the vision of a harvest.

Come over and help us now. (**Acts 16:9**)

Response to this vision saved Europe before.

Your response can touch the world now.